PROPAGATION TECHNIQUES

PROPAGATION TECHNIQUES

Julie Hollobone

NEW HOLLAND

First published in 2008 by New Holland Publishers (UK) Ltd
London • Cape Town • Sydney • Auckland

www.newhollandpublishers.com

Garfield House, 86–88 Edgware Road, London, W2 2EA United Kingdom
80 McKenzie Street, Cape Town, 8001 South Africa
Unit 1, 66 Gibbes Street, Chatswood NSW 2067, Australia
218 Lake Road, Northcote, Auckland New Zealand

ISBN 978 184537 990 2

Commissioning Editor: Clare Sayer
Copy Editor: Jo Smith
Production: Laurence Poos
Design: Nimbus Design
Diagrams: Coral Mula
Editorial Direction: Rosemary Wilkinson

Reproduction by Modern Age Repro House, Hong Kong
Printed and bound in India by Replika Press Pvt. Ltd

10 9 8 7 6 5 4 3 2 1

PHOTOGRAPHY CREDITS
Suttons Seeds: 9, 58, 68, 75, 87, 88, 93, 101, 125, 132, 140, 149, 153
Charlotte de la Bédoyère: 14, 35, 117, 144
Derek St Romaine: 81
Photolibrary Group: 39, 43, 65, 99, 102, 113

CONTENTS

INTRODUCTION

Propagating plants can bring with it a huge sense of achievement when all goes well, but can be demoralising when the results are patchy. Raising plants for yourself can involve patience, dexterity, observation and commitment, but the reward of seeing those first plants grow to maturity is well worth the effort. Suddenly you will start to see plants in a new light, appraising their potential to offer seed or cutting material, and then you will be hooked.

Why propagate?

The obvious answer is that it is cheaper than buying plants as the material is free. It is also a chance to grow a plant variety not normally seen for sale in nurseries or garden centres. It might be an unusual penstemon seen in a neighbour's garden, an old variety of apple on a dying tree or a heritage vegetable not available commercially. However, it can become simply a compulsion for some people because they just love to see new plants start to grow, knowing that they made it happen.

How to propagate

Normally, a plant can be propagated by germinating collected seed or by taking a non-flowering (vegetative) part of the plant and growing roots or shoots from this to produce a new plant in its own right.

Growing crops from collected seeds has been going on for centuries and is very successful, but the seedlings won't all be identical. If you grow aquilegias, for example, it is likely that you also have some self-sown plants appearing in the garden. These might show a mixture of characteristics from cross-pollination between the parents. This is fine when you are happy to enjoy variability, but not when you wish to grow a plant specifically for certain qualities. In this case, using a method of vegetative propagation is the answer. If you have a plant with unusual flower colour, fruit flavour or interesting leaf markings, a suitable method of vegetative propagation will ensure that these qualities are retained in the new plants.

The methods that can be used to propagate plants vary in the degree of skill needed for success, from the easiest, which is probably chopping up a clump-forming hardy perennial into smaller pieces and replanting them, to the more skilled process of grafting a piece of stem onto the stem and root system of a completely different plant. This book offers instructions for both simple and more complex methods.

One of the keys to success with propagation is to observe how the plant is growing. This will help decide which method to use and will also help to identify which parts of the plant provide the best material. Take time to look at a stem and decide if the growth is woody or soft, or keep checking the seed head on a favourite plant so that you are ready to collect the seed when it is shed.

Learning styles

People approach gardening and propagation in different ways. Some beginners just have a go and see what happens, while others may be more cautious and prefer to follow guidelines. The step-by-step instructions in this book will be clear enough for those just wanting to see how it's done.

Gardeners with some experience of propagation but with mixed results will start to think how they can increase success rates and reduce failures. This book has suggestions of what to do if things go wrong, which might help to answer these questions.

Finally, those wishing to know more about the subject will probably enjoy reading about the horticultural principles behind successful propagation. These are clearly explained for all the different propagation methods. Understanding these principles can help the gardener adopt a more instinctive and pragmatic approach to propagation. It's not all about green fingers, it's also about understanding plant structure and maturity.

Regardless of how you use the book, remember that no propagator achieves one hundred per cent success, so don't be disappointed if you have failures. Reflect on what might have been the problem and have another go. You are bound to be successful in the end.

PROPAGATION WITHOUT KNOWING IT

For plants it's all about survival. Once they have found the right place to grow, they use different means to make sure that they can spread over a larger area. They will produce seed in large numbers so that some, at least, will be in the right place to germinate successfully and increase the colony. Along with seeds, they often spread out their stems, putting down roots along the way. These plants are the easiest to propagate, as they virtually do it themselves.

HOW TO USE THIS BOOK

This book can be accessed in different ways:

- If you are a complete beginner, start by learning about different plant types.
- If you have been successful with seeds and cuttings, you might want to read about other methods to try.
- If you have a plant you wish to propagate you can start at the directory to find the best method to follow.

Every gardener plays some part in propagation just by managing those plants in their garden that are most likely to spread and take over. Leaving flowers to develop into seed heads on certain plants will result in new seedlings where the seed falls. If these are recognised and left undisturbed, they can then be transplanted to new positions throughout the garden – a fresh batch of seed-raised plants without any effort.

Often a hardy perennial forms a clump which gets bigger every year. It's easy to chop off a piece to stop its spread, but this can be replanted elsewhere if the roots are left intact. The same goes for a shrub that throws up new shoots from the ground (suckers) as it spreads out. It is easy to dig up one of these and, if roots are attached, it will continue to grow once replanted.

Plants used as groundcover usually grow close to the ground, with an ability to root into fresh soil as they spread. When they spread too far, the stems are cut back. By cutting to ensure that each piece has roots, several new plants can be potted up or planted individually elsewhere.

Just weeding around the base of shrubs might reveal a stem that has rooted into the ground. Several shrubs self-layer in this manner, so rather than pull it out, cut the rooted stem away from the main plant and get a new shrub for free.

When in your own or friends' gardens, be on the look out for potential new plants where they have done the work themselves.

A BIT ABOUT PLANTS

Propagation sounds difficult, but it can be very easy. The idea is to produce new plants from established plants and in nature this happens all the time. Plants that are growing successfully can be observed growing in size but also in their numbers. Take a nettle patch, for example, that successfully spreads by self-propagation normally through spreading underground stems and by casting seed.

Gardeners are always keen to increase numbers of plants that are attractive or useful, and to do this successfully they mimic what plants do naturally but to their own timetable. That is to say, a plant may only propagate itself when conditions happen to be favourable, but gardeners may aim to manipulate the growing conditions to increase the odds in favour of producing many more plants.

To understand propagation, it is useful to understand the variety of plant types, their structure and various life cycles.

Annuals

Annual plants are those that grow from seed and quickly reach a stage where they will flower, usually within weeks when it is warm and wet enough. Insects are attracted to the brightly coloured flowers and so help with pollination, with seeds forming in quick succession. These seeds ripen, fall to the ground and then germinate to form new plants

Pot marigold (Calendula) is an annual plant

when conditions are right. Flowering tails off once seed is produced and plants die shortly after. Annuals are propagated by collecting the seeds before they fall to the ground, and sowing where they are required, maybe in another flowerbed or in a seed tray.

Many wild flowers, a few herbs and all but a few vegetables are annuals, along with many troublesome weeds.

- **Hardy annuals** are those that are able to survive temperatures as low as –5°C (23°F) as plants. If seeds germinate in the late summer, the young plants are able to survive a typical winter. Seeds sown in spring can germinate at soil temperatures of about 10–12°C (50–52°F).
- **Half-hardy annuals** are those that have originated from warmer countries and are not able to survive frosts. They need higher soil temperatures to germinate, usually around 18–20°C (64–68°F). They are often slower to grow and come into flower.

Biennials

These are plants that take slightly longer to flower and produce seed. The plant grows from a germinating seed in the first growing season, but produces the flowering stem and subsequent seed in the second year following a winter chill. Honesty (*Lunaria annua*) and sweet williams (*Dianthus barbatus*) are common garden biennials. A swollen tap root often forms at the end of the first year, and several biennial root vegetables such as carrots and parsnips are harvested at this stage before flowering in the second year. If seeds are required of this crop, then a plant must be left to flower the following year.

Perennials

Perennials are plants that live for more than two years. For gardeners, the term usually refers to non-woody plants, where the top growth dies at the end of the growing year while the roots remain alive but dormant until the temperatures start to rise in the following spring and new shoots appear again. In herbaceous perennials, the top growth dies back completely in winter and is removed to ground level. In some cases a few leaves remain on the plant over winter and these plants may be referred to as **evergreen** perennials. Some stiff-stemmed perennials such as Michaelmas daisies or lupins may appear woody, but the dead stems won't reshoot the following year.

- **Hardy perennials** are those that can tolerate temperatures at or below 0°C (37°F). These perennials would be expected to survive a typical temperate winter.
- **Tender perennials** are those that cannot survive either the regular frosts of winter or the cold combined with winter wet. Many plants used for bedding or patio containers are tender perennials. They can survive for many years if given suitable winter protection, such as that offered by a frost-free greenhouse.
- **Bulbs** True bulbs are perennial plants where the top growth is seasonal, but the bulb remains alive and dormant underground until the following year. It has the same structural parts as other plants, but the stem is reduced to a small plate above the roots, onto which fleshy leaves are attached. These swell as they store food to fuel the new leaves and flower stem when they appear above ground. In garden borders, the flowers on bulbs such as daffodils are welcome, but in the vegetable garden bulbs such as onions are harvested when the underground leaves are swollen but before flowers appear. Bulbs can be grown from seed, but growth is slow.
- **Other bulbous plants** There are other non-woody perennials that behave like bulbs in that they grow from a part of the plant that is swollen and acts as a food store. These may be root tubers, stem tubers or swollen underground stems known as rhizomes. An effective method to propagate these plants is to cut the storage structures into sections and encourage roots and shoots to develop.
- **Woody perennials** These are typically the trees and shrubs in the garden that grow to form a permanent woody framework on which new shoots emerge each year. The leaves may fall from the framework in autumn but new shoots will generally appear in spring on the bare stems above ground. Garden trees and shrubs can vary in hardiness, depending on their place of origin.

Perennial plants will grow from seed, but the rate at which they mature varies. It depends on how quickly the seed will germinate and grow into a reasonably sized mature plant ready to produce flowers and seeds itself. There are other methods that have been found to be quicker and more successful depending on how the plants grow.

Plant structure

A typical plant has a fibrous root system growing out of a single stem at the base. Higher up the plant, the main stem might branch out into several stem tips where new leaf buds and occasionally flower buds form. A shrub such as lavender would be a typical example. Although it wouldn't happen naturally, gardeners have found that many plants with this structure can be propagated by taking lengths of the stem and encouraging them to grow fresh roots.

However, not all plants grow in this manner. Many shrubs throw up several stems from below soil level that already have roots growing from them; these can just be severed from the main plant and replanted. Many hardy perennials and ornamental grasses don't grow with a single main stem but with many leaves and stems arising from a fibrous original.

Many plants store food in different structures as a survival strategy to overcome the challenges of winter. These swollen structures may have originally been stem or root but can often be cut from the main plant and encouraged to grow into new individual plants. Swollen stems such as rhizomes, bulbs and corms can be cut into sections and produce new plants far faster than growing the same plants from seed. All these techniques and many others will be described in this book.

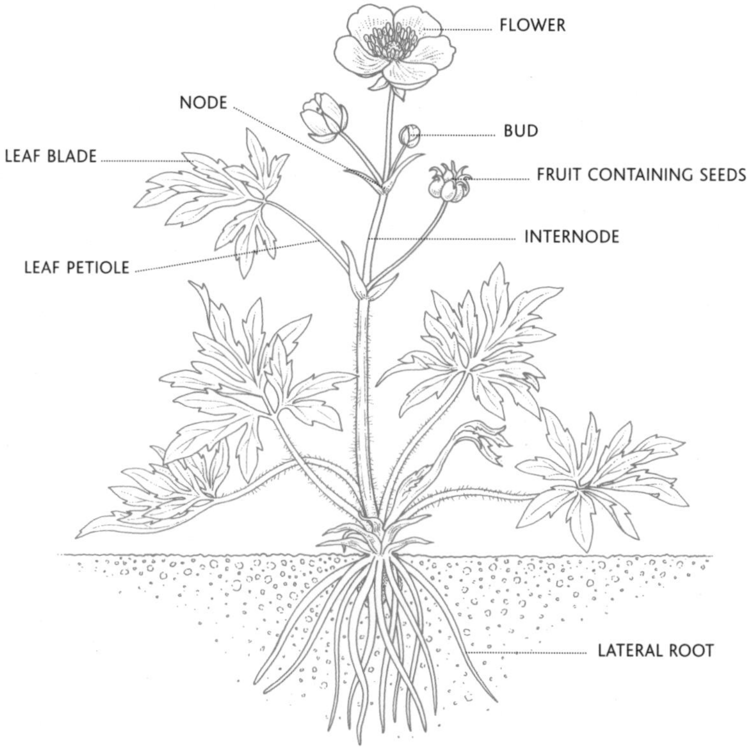

GROWING PLANTS FROM SEED

What could be more satisfying than watching the seeds that you've sown burst into life and develop into a swathe of new plants for the garden? Getting seeds to germinate can be as easy as sprinkling a few mustard seeds onto damp tissue and waiting for a couple of days. However, not all seeds are so ready to sprout and many require a more complex set of conditions before they will germinate. This is to ensure that when the seeds do germinate, the resulting plants have a good chance of survival. It's great fun to try and get all sorts of seeds to germinate, but if you have failures remember that some are easier than others.

Plants flower in order to produce seed to ensure the continued survival of the species. Seed is usually produced in large numbers so there is a plentiful supply for germination. In nature, this allows for a proportion of the seed to land where it is unlikely to germinate and grow.

Plants grown from seed usually resemble the parent plants but there will always be some variation. Often this is slight, but sometimes a batch of seed will throw up something a little more different. This natural variation helps the population to continue. Within the mix, there will be some plants better suited to any changes in environmental conditions that may occur. These particular plants can grow on and flower, passing on their strengths to the next generation of seeds and allowing the species to survive.

Growing plants from seed successfully involves careful collection and storage of the seed. Sowing the seeds outdoors is simpler, but losses are usually greater. Raising the seeds under cover requires more attention being paid to the plants before they are planted out, but is generally more successful as the growing conditions can be tightly controlled. Both methods have their uses, and the best choice depends on what type of plant you want to grow and what equipment you have available.

FROM FLOWER TO SEED

Apart from a few plants such as ferns and mosses, all garden plants produce flowers at some stage in their life. The aim of a flower is to produce seeds to continue the line. Even plants grown for their foliage will produce flowers, but they may be small and inconspicuous. Most annual plants reach a flowering stage after only weeks of growth, but it may be many years before certain trees and shrubs reach flowering maturity.

The sequence of events that occurs before a plant produces seed is complicated and requires a large input of energy. A seed is a concentrated packet of information stored in a weatherproof jacket.

Flower structure

A typical flower contains both male and female parts. In the centre of the flower is the female part comprising an ovary containing ovules (or eggs) that contain the genetic information. Surrounding the ovary are the male parts of the flower, comprising many stamens with anthers at the tip containing genetic information in the numerous grains of pollen. Surrounding these vital structures are the petals, often highly coloured and of various shapes and sizes. In some plants the male and female parts are held in separate flowers. This can be separate flowers on the same plant, for example hazel, or flowers on separate plants, such as holly, skimmia, pernettya and *Viburnum davidii*.

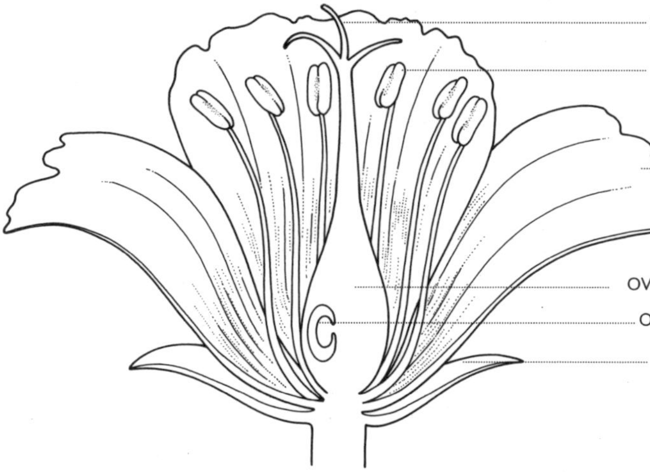

POLLINATION

To produce seed, a flower has to be pollinated. This happens when pollen is transferred from the anthers (the male part) of one flower to the stigma (the female part) of another flower of the same species, thus bringing together the genetic information from both flowers. Self-pollination occurs when pollen is transferred between two flowers on the same plant. Cross-pollination occurs when the pollen is transferred between flowers on two different plants of the same species.

Seed and fruit structure

When a pollen grain lands on the surface of the stigma, it moves towards the ovary and fuses with an ovule to form a single plant cell. The cell divides several times to form a cluster of many cells known as an embryo. This will go on to develop into a seed, containing an embryonic shoot and root plus a store of food, all encased in a protective seed coat called a testa. In the meantime, the former ovary of the flower develops into a fruit designed to nurture the developing seeds.

Seeds come in many shapes and sizes and are contained within fruits of many shapes and sizes. The type of fruit a plant produces is related to the structure of the original flower, which in turn varies between plant families. Some fruits have soft, fleshy walls, others are drier and are often referred to as seed cases or seed pods.

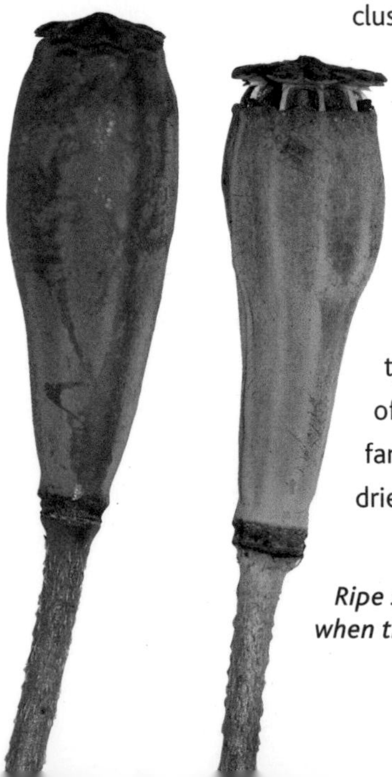

Ripe seed pods usually turn brown when they are ready to harvest.

Some fruits contain only one seed (for example a cherry), but others contain hundreds (for example a poppy seed head). Take this into account when considering how many fruits to collect to gain a good supply of seed.

If you are aiming to collect seeds to raise plants for the garden, it is useful to become familiar with the variety of different forms fruits can take. The more you look around at different plants, the easier it will be to recognise the developing seed case and work out how the seed might be shed. In many cases, the structure and method of seed dispersal go hand in hand.

WINGED SEEDS

The seeds are held in a flat case extended to form a 'wing'. A good example is the seed of sycamore. The wing allows the seed to fly some distance to germinate in an area where there is less competition from the parent tree.

SEEDS IN PODS AND CASES THAT SPLIT OPEN

The seed is held in the case until it is mature, at which time the seed case splits open to allow the seeds to disperse. Some cases split under tension and expel seeds away from the parent plant. A good example is busy lizzie (*Impatiens*).

SEEDS ON PARACHUTES OR IN FLUFF

These small, light seeds can be more easily carried on the wind to fresh ground, particularly with the aid of fine hairs. Good examples are the seeds of dandelions and some clematis species.

SEEDS THAT STICK

Sometimes the seed has a sticky substance to help its dispersal, like mistletoe seeds sticking to the beaks of birds. Alternatively, the seed coat can have hooks which attach to animal fur. In both these cases the seed hitches a lift to fresh ground.

SEEDS IN FLESHY FRUITS

The sweet flesh attracts birds, which eat the fruits. The seeds are later excreted unharmed and at some distance from the parent plant.

SEEDS IN CONES

Hard and heavy cones bounce and roll when they fall from a tree, allowing the seeds inside to slip out some distance from the parent plant.

SEED GERMINATION

As a seed develops in the flower, it prepares for what may be a long and challenging period in the soil waiting for conditions to be just right for germination. In many plants, seeds are produced in mid to late summer, so the ideal time for these seeds to germinate is either immediately before temperatures fall, or in the spring as soil temperatures rise again. Different plants employ different strategies to ensure that the seed germinates at the optimum time, and formation of a tough seed coat around the embryo plant will give some protection until this time comes. In most cases the embryo will lose moisture and enter a period of very low activity while waiting for the right conditions. In this state, seeds can survive for long periods, which is why they should be stored in dry conditions for long-term preservation.

The process of germination

When all the correct factors are in place, a seed will germinate. This begins with the seed absorbing water through the seed coat. As the water is absorbed, the seed swells and the coat starts to split. The root of the seedling, the radicle, will emerge first. It will grow downwards regardless of which way up the seed is placed as it responds to gravity.

Next the shoots appear in one of two ways. Contained within the seed are the cotyledons or food stores which provide energy for growth. Most ornamental flowering plants have two cotyledons, but grasses and bulbous plants have just one.

In Epigeal germination, the cotyledons are pushed out from the seed case and emerge above ground first, appearing as two rounded 'seed leaves'. The 'true leaves', which show the characteristics of the plant, appear after the seed leaves. Sometimes the seed case might stick to the seed leaves as they emerge and you may want to flick these off to help germination on its way.

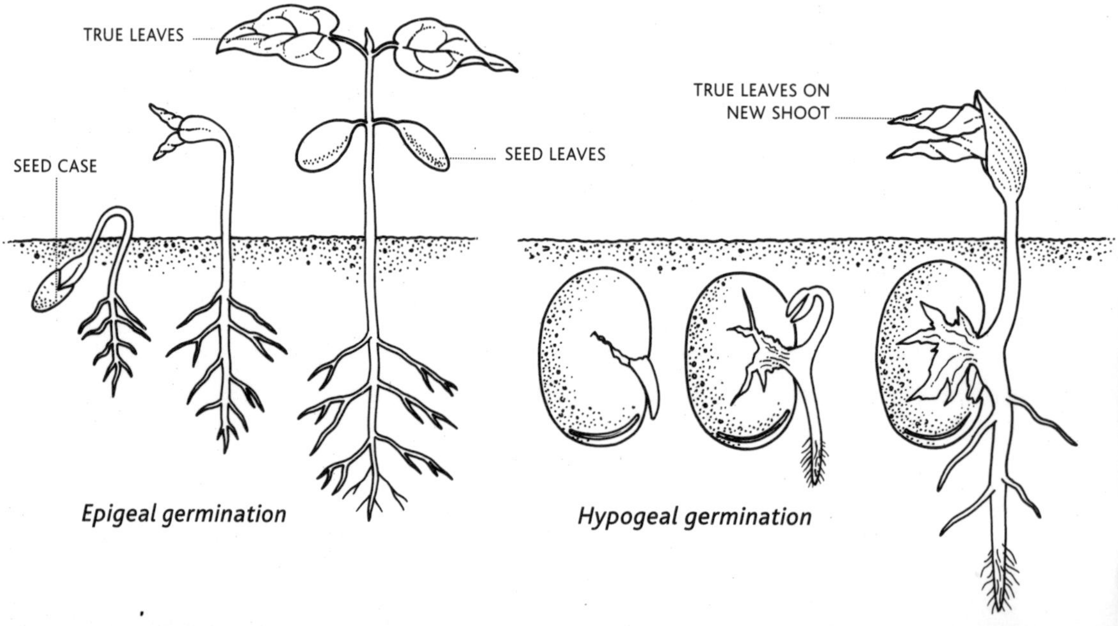

Epigeal germination

Hypogeal germination

CONDITIONS FOR SEED GERMINATION

MOISTURE • The seed needs to be in a moist environment to rehydrate the embryo within, so that the process of growth can begin.

FOOD • The process of cell division and growth will require a source of food to act as a fuel and this is contained in the seed embryo itself in the form of starch, fats or proteins.

OXYGEN • Complex food structures are broken down to release energy for growth. Oxygen is required for this process and is normally found in a well aerated compost or similar growing medium.

TEMPERATURE • The process of seed germination and growth increases with an increase in temperature. Initial germination of seeds of hardy plants will take place at lower temperatures than those originating from warmer climates.

VIABILITY OF THE SEED • If seeds have been damaged externally or internally, for example through disease, this may not be apparent at the time of sowing, however, germination will be poor.

In Hypogeal germination, the cotyledons remain in the seed case and the developing shoot, the plumule, emerges first followed by the foliage leaves. Seeds of grasses and bulbs germinate in this manner but with only one foliage leaf appearing.

Growth begins

A seed contains only enough energy to push the first leaves into the light. From this point, the leaves turn green and begin to photosynthesise, manufacturing all further supplies of food that the growing seedling will require. It is therefore important that seeds are not planted too deep in the soil or compost, otherwise the supply of food will have been expended before the leaves reach the light. Big seeds such as broad beans have a greater food store and can be pushed further into the compost or soil. Fine seed has minimal food reserves so it must be at or just below the surface to germinate and grow on successfully.

Even when the seed has started to grow it is still very fragile. The newly formed leaves need a good light level to photosynthesise and produce energy, but they can easily scorch in strong sunlight and any damage would reduce the food production so necessary for growth. Similarly, the delicate leaves and roots of the seedling will collapse and die if they are allowed to dry out so the compost or soil must be kept moist.

Many seedlings fail at this stage but the gardener can reduce the losses by keeping seedlings constantly warm and moist in a bright position but shaded from strong sun. Looking after seedlings once they have germinated will result in sturdy plants later on.

SOWING SEED OUTDOORS

If you don't have a greenhouse or windowsill, there are plenty of plants that can be started off from seed sown outdoors. You will have less control over creating the right conditions for germination and subsequent growth, so expect to encounter more losses. However, you can compensate by sowing more seeds than you need, and using a variety of crop covers to create more favourable conditions. Due to its ease and simplicity, many gardeners start off by sowing seed direct into garden soil, and there are tricks to attaining greater success.

Equipment

- A **rake** is useful to break down large clods of soil and prepare a fine soil crumb (tilth). It can also be used to cover seeds with soil after sowing.
- A **hoe** can be used to create a shallow trough into which to sow the seeds.
- A **garden line** can be used as a guide to follow when making a seed drill or sowing seeds in rows.
- A **dibber** can be used to create deep holes into which larger seeds can be dropped.
- **Labels** should be used to identify the position of crops sown. This will tell you which are the seedlings and which are the weeds.
- **Crop covers** create favourable conditions close to the soil by reducing wind and trapping warm air, although extra irrigation may be necessary. They may also offer some protection from pests when seedlings emerge. A cloche is usually a rigid structure covered by glass, polythene or polycarbonate used to cover the soil or the crop where needed. However, polythene sheeting and fleece can be simply laid over newly sown seed for protection.

WHAT TO SOW OUTDOORS

HARDY ANNUALS, such as love-in-a-mist (Nigella), clarkia and pot marigold (Calendula), create a quick, bright patch of colour in the border. Sow into small patches of bare garden soil where they won't be overcrowded by other plants later in the year.

HARDY BIENNIALS produce flowers in the following year. Try sowing foxgloves (Digitalis purpurea) or honesty (Lunaria annua).

HARDY VEGETABLES can be sown in rows in the vegetable patch. These include carrots, beetroot and spinach.

TENDER VEGETABLES, such as green beans and runner beans, can be sown outdoors once soil temperatures are high enough (usually by June).

SLOW-GROWING VEGETABLES, such as cabbages or leeks, are sometimes sown in a separate patch of ground and then transplanted to their final positions in the vegetable garden when space becomes available.

When to sow

SPRING

In general, March is the earliest time you can sow hardy annuals and hardy vegetables, but it does depend on the weather conditions in preceding weeks. Very few seeds germinate in cold, dank soil, but get going once soil temperatures increase as the sun gets stronger. A very cold spell won't affect seeds just sown, but may kill off young seedlings which have already germinated so that a fresh batch will need to be sown.

A cloche will warm a patch of soil prior to sowing and can then be kept in place to protect the new seedlings from extremes of weather. If it's very cold, delay sowing until the weather is warmer as the seedlings will get off to a better start.

SUMMER

Sow tender vegetables in early June. Vegetable crops which are quick to mature, such as lettuce, rocket and radishes, can be sown at regular intervals until about August, but they will struggle if it is very hot and dry through the summer months. Hardy biennials like foxgloves can be sown in summer to flower the following year.

AUTUMN

Some flowering hardy annuals such as sweet peas and calendula can be sown in September. The young plants will overwinter and flower early the following year. However, some plants may be lost in bad winters. Winter salads can be sown in early autumn and covered with a cloche. Sow broad beans in the open.

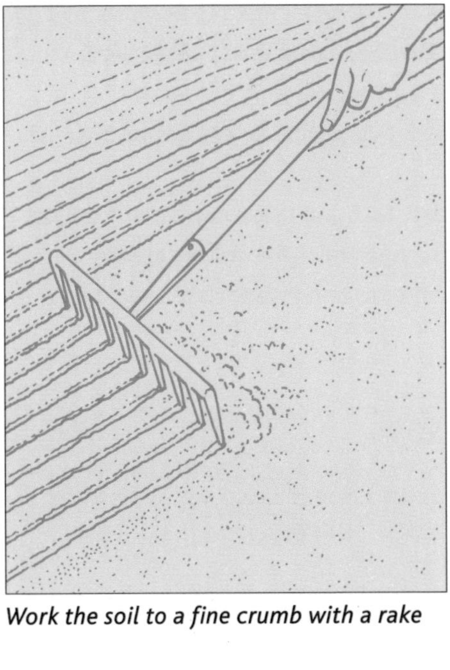

Work the soil to a fine crumb with a rake

Soil requirements

Seeds can be sown outdoors onto a small patch of bare earth between established plants, a specially prepared seed bed from where they are transplanted to their final growing position, or directly into a bare soil bed such as in a vegetable garden or allotment. A previously unused patch of soil will require the most preparation to achieve a suitable tilth for seeds.

PREPARING A FINE TILTH

For germinating seeds to push through to the surface, the soil needs to be worked to create a fine crumb where most soil lumps are the size of hazelnuts or less. The smaller the seeds, the smaller the shoots they produce and the less able they are to displace heavy lumps of soil in their efforts to reach the surface. So the fineness of the tilth required is in part related to the size of the seed being sown.

Start by digging the soil over when it is neither too wet nor too dry, using a garden spade or fork. If the soil naturally breaks down to a texture like breadcrumbs it is ideal for seed germination and needs no extra cultivation. If after digging the soil is sitting in large lumps, these need to be broken down further through a combination of turning the soil surface with a garden fork and using a garden rake. Use the fork to spear the lumps, turn them over and smash them into smaller pieces. Use the rake to move the soil forwards and backwards to break down the lumps, but don't rake off the larger lumps; instead use the rake head to break these down to a smaller size.

Once the soil crumb comprises a mix of lumps from the size of breadcrumbs up to hazelnuts it is ready for sowing.

WEED CONTROL

Any cultivation will bring weed seeds to the soil surface which will thrive in the care and attention given to the site once the desired seeds are sown. If you have the time, leave the site for two weeks or so after preparation until the weed seeds germinate, then remove them by hoeing the soil surface. Try not to disturb the soil too much or more weed seeds will be brought to the surface causing a further flush of growth.

Sowing depth

A germinating seed only has sufficient food stores to push the first leaves up through the soil into the light. A small seed has a far smaller food store than a larger seed. Therefore, a seed will only successfully grow into a strong seedling if it is sown at the correct depth. A good rule is to cover the seed with a depth of soil equivalent to double its own size.

Very fine seed can be left on the soil surface but take great care not to let it dry out. Small seeds such as foxgloves or lettuce should be just under the soil surface for successful germination, while large seeds like courgettes and broad beans should be 2.5–5 cm (1–2 in) deep.

HOW TO SOW

Prepare the soil • Sow the seed at the correct depth • Cover the seed with soil • Water the soil thoroughly, using a fine spray on small seeds • Label the area with the name of the plant and the date of sowing

Sowing methods

Different methods of sowing suit different types of plants and the way they are to be used in the garden.

BROADCASTING SEED

Distribute the seed onto the surface of the soil in a random pattern and leave it where it falls. Cover the seed lightly with soil by gently drawing a rake over the area.

- **Uses:** small seeds such as lawn grass seed, hardy annuals or quick-growing salad vegetables.
- **Advantages:** gives a natural appearance. Results in a more uniform cover of seed, useful in lawns.
- **Disadvantages:** seedlings may need to be thinned. It can be difficult to identify weeds in some cases, and difficult to remove weeds either with a hoe or by hand without disturbing the seedlings.

SOWING IN DRILLS

Sow the seeds in marked rows. To get the correct depth, make a narrow furrow by drawing a cane or the edge of a hoe along the soil against a straight board. Once the furrow is made to the same depth all along its length, the seeds can be dropped into the base of the drill at regular intervals. Draw the soil back over the seeds using the hoe or rake and then firm gently.

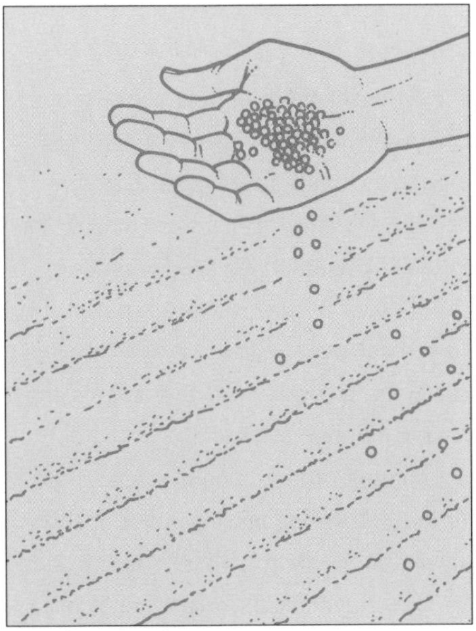

Broadcasting seed

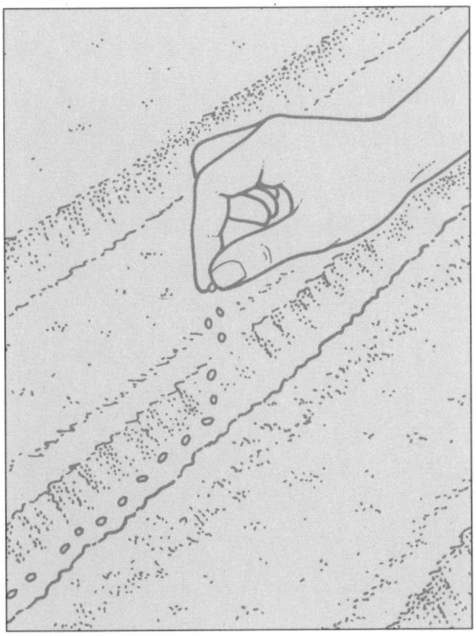

Sowing into drills

- **Uses:** for larger seeds in the vegetable garden, for seeds to be grown on before transplanting to a final position, or for hardy annuals in flower beds.
- **Advantages:** any seedlings that emerge outside the line of the drill can be assumed to be weeds and removed early on.
- **Disadvantages:** it is possible to sow some seeds too deeply.

STATION SOWING

Sow the seeds at the correct spacing in their final growing positions. Make a single hole in the soil and drop in one or two seeds, then cover them with soil. If both seeds germinate successfully, remove one of them early on to avoid competition.

- **Uses:** larger seeds like nasturtiums (*Tropaeolum majus*) or vegetables seeds such as beans, courgettes or pumpkins.
- **Advantages:** seeds are sown in their final positions and don't require transplanting. There is little seed wastage.
- **Disadvantages:** if a seed doesn't germinate, you have to start again.

Aftercare

Water the soil thoroughly after sowing. If necessary, cover the soil with a cloche or horticultural fleece to keep the soil warm and to prevent birds taking the seeds close to the surface. As seedlings appear, keep the soil well watered. If necessary, introduce slug controls early on.

Thin seedlings to give them space to grow

Thinning

Once the seedlings appear above ground, they need sufficient space to develop properly. Usually, more seeds than are needed will have been sown to allow for losses. If the emerging seedlings are closely packed, you will need to remove some of them to allow a greater spacing. Seedlings become weak and lanky if they are not thinned sufficiently.

Thinning can be done in stages, with an initial thinning leaving some of the unwanted seedlings still in place to allow for subsequent losses due to pests or poor weather. Thin again as the seedlings

SIMPLE TRICKS

If the soil is too warm Some seeds, such as lettuce, germinate poorly at temperatures above 20°C (68°F). If the soil is warm and dry through summer, delay sowing until the evening, then thoroughly water the base of the sowing drill prior to sowing as normal. The cool moist conditions will last overnight, hopefully long enough for a successful germination.

If the soil is too cold Gardeners can find it difficult to germinate parsley seeds sown directly into soil early in the year. Soil temperatures need to be at 15°C (59°F) or above, so try pouring near-boiling water along the drill just prior to sowing the seed and then cover well to retain the heat.

WHAT CAN GO WRONG

SEEDLINGS DON'T EMERGE

Problem: seeds are too old and not viable
Action: check the collection or use-by dates on seed packets

Problem: soil is too cold
Action: use a soil thermometer. Delay sowing seed if the soil is cold and wet, as this can cause seed to rot

Problem: seeds are sown too deeply
Action: dig down to see if the seeds have germinated but failed to reach the surface. Check the depth of seed drills

Problem: soil structure is too coarse
Action: ensure the soil is worked to a fine tilth. Alternatively raise plants in modules and plant out later

Problem: soil is too dry at sowing and immediately afterwards
Action: water regularly and thoroughly. Cover the soil with a cloche to retain moisture

SEEDLINGS EMERGE AND THEN DIE BACK OR DISAPPEAR

Problem: seedlings damaged by pests
Action: use controls against slugs and snails. Try barriers against birds

grow larger to give them enough space to develop fully. Simply pull the unwanted seedlings out of the soil by their leaves, working carefully to avoid disturbing the roots of the seedlings around them.

SOWING SEED UNDER COVER

Many plants can be started off indoors on a windowsill, in a conservatory or in a heated or unheated greenhouse. Each situation provides slightly different growing conditions which may suit some plants better than others. Trial and error will show where the greatest degree of success lies.

Why sow under cover?

When starting off seeds under cover, environmental conditions can be controlled to increase the chance of successful germination. The temperature can be raised to suit more tender plants, and speeds up the process of germination for vulnerable seeds. The moisture levels in compost can be more closely controlled to avoid losses by waterlogging or drying out. If seeds are sown in sterile compost rather than in the open garden, they are much less vulnerable to soil pests or diseases. Finally, many gardeners find it easier to monitor the progress of their seeds when they are all together and easy to see.

Another advantage of sowing under cover is that some tender plants can be sown much earlier if the environment is heated and so get an early start for summer. However, light levels will still be low, so good growth will only be achieved where there is natural light overhead or specialized supplementary lighting.

Equipment needed

Many seeds will germinate without any special equipment but others, often from warmer climates, need a little more attention if they are to be coaxed into life. You may have far fewer seeds to work with, so a good rate of success is more important. Many items of seed-raising equipment are designed to give more control over the process and provide the seeds with the best possible conditions in which to germinate.

- **Seed trays** These are good for sowing seeds in large numbers. Trays are usually shallow, as the seed roots in the first few days are only small. The drainage holes stop seeds from rotting off in wet compost. Trays are available in standard, half and quarter sizes.
- **Modules** These are plastic inserts of various sizes which sit in a seed tray and divide it into individual plugs of soil to house individual seeds. The individual root systems are less prone to damage during potting on.
- **Pots** These are suitable for sowing large seeds individually or in pairs. The extra depth

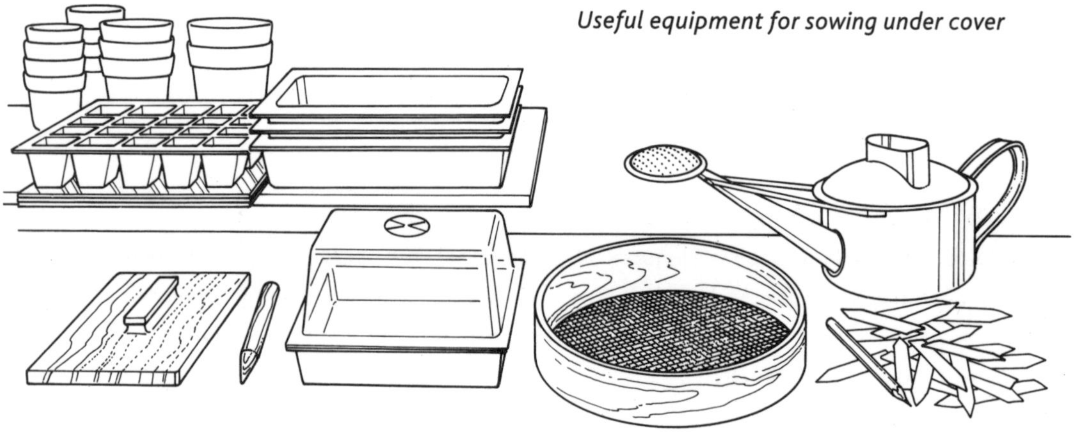

Useful equipment for sowing under cover

suits a larger root system. Standard 9 cm (3½ in) pots are the ideal size.

- **Seed covers** These are used to cover the compost and retain moisture after sowing. There is a wide range of options available (see below).
- **Propagator** A moulded tray with a moulded cover into which one or several seed trays can be placed. The tray collects drainage water from the compost and the tight cover will retain moisture and raise the temperature a little to speed germination. Electric heated propagators will maintain a consistent temperature of your choice.
- **Tamper** Used to lightly firm the compost in a pot or seed tray before sowing the seed. They are especially useful if cut to the same size as the container.

CHOOSING A SEED TRAY COVER

GLASS SHEETS • Traditionally used to cover seed trays. However, they don't allow much space for the seedlings to develop and must be removed soon after germination.

CLING FILM • A lighter and more disposable cover.

FLEECE • Does not retain water so well, but can provide shading too.

MOULDED CLEAR PLASTIC COVERS • These are available to cover seed trays, half trays or pots. They usually allow space for seeds to grow up to at least 5 cm (2 in) high so have a longer period of usefulness.

HEATED PROPAGATORS

Keeping the seeds at a consistent temperature can greatly increase your success at germination. The base trays of electric heated propagators contain heating wires to increase the compost temperature and keep it fixed. Propagators can be found to suit all spaces, from a narrow windowsill to a large greenhouse bench. You will need an electric socket close by. There are two types of propagator:

FIXED HEAT • The temperature is preset, usually at 20°C (68°F), which is suitable for most seeds.

VARIABLE HEAT • The temperature in the base can be adjusted to suit the ideal germination temperatures of different seeds.

SEED TREATMENTS

The following equipment may be useful for seeds which require special treatments to aid germination.

KNIFE • to pierce hard seed coats before sowing.

SAND PAPER IN A JAM JAR • to break down hard seed coats by abrasion.

HOT WATER • to presoak seeds before sowing.

- **Sieve** A coarse sieve can be used to remove large lumps from the compost if you are sowing fine seed. A finer sieve can be used to apply a light dusting of fine compost over small seeds after sowing.
- **Dibber/widger** Used to dig down under the seed roots when pricking out, and to make a hole in the compost for transplanting seedlings. A pencil or stick can do the job, but a plastic version can be washed and sterilized if required.
- **Labels** These can be bought or made, but they need to be waterproof.
- **Pen/pencil** A labelling pen is ideal as the ink is both clear and durable, but a pencil is adequate.
- **Watering can** This should have a fine rose attached to deliver a light shower of water. A water mister could be used as an alternative.

Choosing a compost

Seeds are able to germinate without soil or compost, but for a seedling to grow on successfully, the roots must remain moist as they spread and be able to provide anchorage and support for the developing plant.

There are many materials and commercial composts to choose from but whatever you choose should possess the following properties:

- It must hold onto some water, but let the excess drain away so that seeds are kept moist but not waterlogged.
- It must have a light, fine texture so that the fragile seedling shoots can easily push their way through to the surface.
- It should be sterile so that the seedlings are not weakened by tiny pests, diseases or copious weed seedlings.

COMPOST TYPES

There are two main types of compost which can be used to sow seeds.

SEED/CUTTINGS COMPOST • This is formulated specifically for starting off seeds and cuttings, but is not good for growing on young plants. It has a fine texture and low nutrient levels as these are not required for initial growth. This type of compost is usually more expensive, so often only used by those doing a lot of propagation.

MULTI-PURPOSE COMPOST • As its name suggests, this type of compost will suit a large number of uses. The texture may be slightly coarser but it will contain sufficient nutrients to sustain young plants for about six weeks after germination. It is cheaper and more versatile as the same bag can be used for germinating seeds and growing on young plants as they mature.

COMPOST COMPONENTS

The main component of a compost can vary but is usually peat, a peat substitute, or a combination of soil and peat.

- **Soil-less composts** The main component is frequently peat but it can also be coir, wood fibre, recycled municipal green waste or a combination of any of these. The organic content is high but the water retention and fine texture can be variable, depending on the mix. Soil-less composts are light to handle, sterile and hold moisture well, but they are difficult to rewet if allowed to dry out in the seed tray or pot.
- **Soil-based composts** These contain roughly 60 per cent loam and 40 per cent peat or peat substitute for raising seeds. The loam component is soil made up of a mix of sand, silt and clay to give an ideal growing medium. Soil-based composts may be too coarse for fine seeds, but suit larger seeds needing good anchorage. They are heavier than soil-less composts and therefore more expensive.

RECYCLED MATERIALS

Some materials can be used from the garden to make composts, but with possible problems.

- **Garden soil** This can vary in its sand, silt and clay content, so it may have a coarse or fine crumb and could be either well or poorly drained. Garden soil isn't sterile and is likely to contain weed seeds and other harmful agents which may cause losses.
- **Garden compost** Homemade compost can be sieved to make it finer, but its sterility will depend on whether the compost has reached a high enough temperature to destroy weed seeds and diseases.
- **Leafmould** Once the leaves have rotted down to a fine crumb, leafmould can be sieved to make it finer, but although it's unlikely to hold weed seeds, fungal disease organisms could be a problem to seedlings.

MINOR COMPONENTS

Just as different plants prefer soils with different drainage properties, so seeds can benefit from different rooting media.

- **Fine grit or coarse sand** This creates a more open texture in a compost and improves drainage – especially important for trees and shrubs.
- **Coarse grit** This is better for covering the compost and reducing the growth of mosses or lichens, for use with seeds that are slow to germinate.
- **Vermiculite** This pale brown expanded mica is available in fine, medium and coarse

WHAT TO SOW UNDER COVER

Hardy annuals, half-hardy annuals and tender perennials for bedding and patio pots • Hardy perennials and bulbs, especially those with very fine seed • Houseplants, including cacti • Trees and shrubs where only a few seeds are available • Hardy vegetables that tolerate transplanting • Tender vegetables • Hardy and tender herbs.

grades. The fine grade can be used as a compost additive to help with drainage and aeration of the compost. The medium grade is often used to cover fine seeds after they are surface sown as it helps with water retention but allows light to reach the seeds.

When to sow

LATE WINTER

Sow half-hardy annuals and tender perennials if a temperature of 18–21°C (64–70°F) can be maintained during the day, with night temperatures of 10–15°C (50–59°F). By starting these plants early, they will be in full flower in May when temperatures are high enough for them to grow outside.

Many hardy perennials can be sown in February to achieve early maturity and the possibility of flowering in the first year of growth. Hardy salads can be sown and grown on to harvest undercover during the winter.

SPRING

As light levels increase, virtually any seed can be started off on the windowsill or in a heated greenhouse, but an unheated position will still be too cold at night for tender plants. Wait until March or April to sow without heat, depending on the weather in your area.

SUMMER

This is a good time to sow slower growing hardy perennials, bulbs, shrubs and trees when the pressure for space in spring has eased. This is also the time to start off winter bedding plants such as pansies.

AUTUMN

Sow hardy annuals such as sweet peas to be overwintered as young plants. Sow plants whose seeds need a winter chill before they will germinate, such as hellebore, anemone and many trees and shrubs originating from cold climates.

Sowing seed in a container

Prepare the compost by breaking down any large lumps between the palms of the hands. Fill a clean container to the rim with compost, taking care to fill the corners. Tap the container down firmly to remove air pockets. Level off the top surface with a straight edge like a cane or tamper held on its side. Gently firm the compost using a tamper. If you wish, water the compost and leave to drain.

Sow seeds thinly and evenly on the surface and cover with a thin layer of compost. Label and water the compost with a fine spray if you haven't already done so. Cover the tray with a sheet of glass, clingfilm or propagator lid to retain moisture. If the cover is airtight, the seeds will need no further watering until after they have germinated. If the trays are left in a sunny position, use newspaper or shading material to prevent seedlings scorching in the sun.

Remove the glass or clingfilm cover as seedlings appear. Water the compost more frequently to prevent it drying out.

Pricking out

Often seeds are sown too closely together to grow on without competing for light and space, so they should be transplanted into fresh trays of compost at a greater spacing. This should be done as soon as the seedlings can be handled, which may be at the seed leaf stage of larger seedlings, or with two or more sets of true leaves if the seedlings are very small.

Fill a fresh tray with fresh compost to the rim. Loosen the compost around the seedlings by inserting a dibber below the roots to allow you to lift out individual

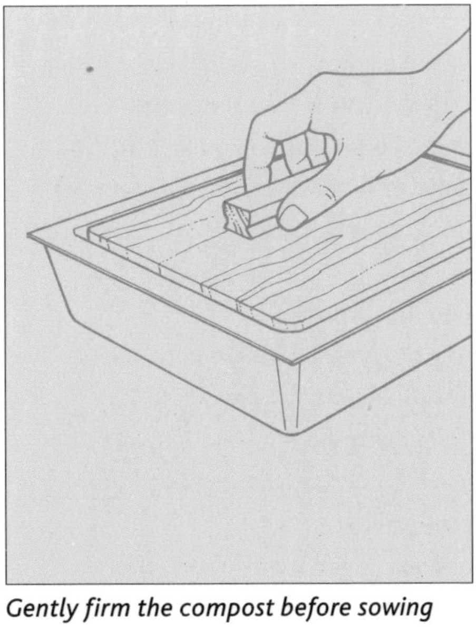

Gently firm the compost before sowing

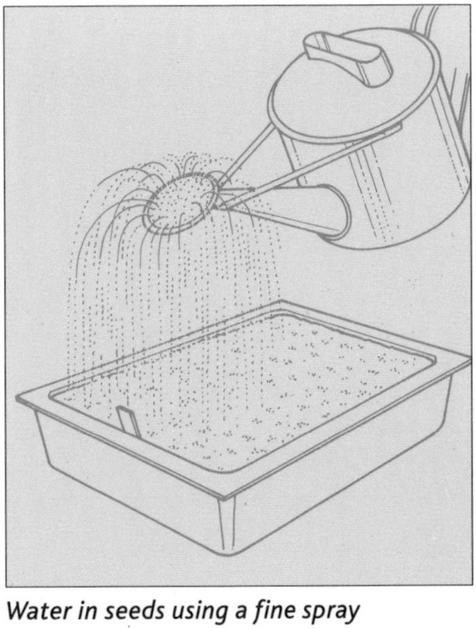

Water in seeds using a fine spray

seedlings. Always handle seedlings by their leaves as the young stems are easily damaged at this stage. Using the dibber, make a hole in the fresh tray to accommodate the seedling roots, then gently lower it in so that it sits with the first leaves at compost level. Use the dibber to gently push compost back around the stem.

Prick out as many further seedlings as you need in the same way into rows across the tray so that the seedlings are evenly spaced in both directions. The seedlings can be pricked out in rows of 7 x 5 or 6 x 4 in a standard tray, depending on how quickly the seedlings will grow on to fill the space. Water the trays to allow the compost to settle around the roots.

USEFUL TIP

If your batch of seed contains plants with a mixture of flower colours, some colours may be weaker than others. To make sure you don't end up with just one colour, prick out some small and some large seedlings so that the final plants will reflect the full range of the mix.

Aftercare

Once seedlings have germinated, they can often be moved to a cooler position. It must be well lit so that seedlings grow compact and strong, but out of direct sun to avoid damage by scorching. If you are using a propagator, this will free up space for fresh batches of seeds.

Remove covers if seedling leaves are touching them. This will allow the compost to dry out more quickly so check it regularly thereafter. The compost should be moist but not waterlogged.

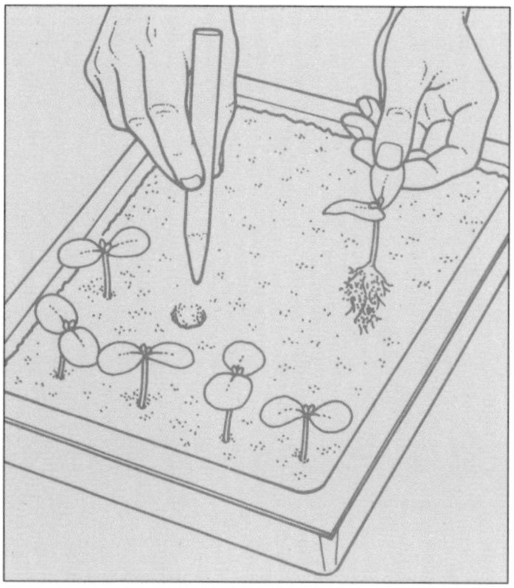

Prick out seedlings to give them space to grow

Check seedlings daily and water them as required. When plants begin to look crowded in the tray, they need to be prepared for planting outside. If the weather is still too cold, pot them on into individual pots.

Hardening off

Any plant raised in the protected environment of a windowsill, conservatory or greenhouse will not be used to outdoor growing conditions or cool nights.

Plants need to be acclimatized steadily over a few days before they can be left outside. Hardy plants can be hardened off to lower temperatures but they might not survive a night of frost immediately after being taken out of the greenhouse. Half-hardy and tender plants can be hardened off once the danger of frosts has passed.

To harden off, place plants in a sheltered site outside during the day but return to their original home at night for several days. Then leave them outside overnight in the sheltered position for a few days before planting out into their final growing positions. A cold frame can be a useful halfway step from a heated environment to outdoors.

WHAT CAN GO WRONG

SEEDLINGS DON'T APPEAR

Problem: seeds too old and not viable
Action: check seed storage conditions and the date they were packed or collected

Problem: compost is too wet
Action: touch the compost to check if it is moist enough each time before watering. Mix perlite or vermiculite into the compost to aid drainage

Problem: temperature is too hot or too cold for germination
Action: use a soil thermometer. Check the thermostat on propagator. Check temperature requirements of the seed

SEEDLINGS APPEAR THEN COLLAPSE

Problem: seedlings suffered from sun scorch
Action: move seeds to a well lit but shaded position. Create a shaded area using fleece, shading material or greenhouse shading paint as appropriate

Problem: seedlings attacked by the fungal disease known as damping off
Action: sow again using fresh compost and clean containers. Sow more thinly and take care not to overwater. Consider watering in Cheshunt compound, a fungicide, after sowing

Problem: seedlings attacked by tiny scarid fly that move when the container is disturbed
Action: use fresh compost and clean trays and resow

SEEDLINGS BECOME ELONGATED AND THIN

Problem: seedlings overcrowded and need thinning
Action: prick out seedlings immediately and grow on in bright conditions or resow

Problem: compost temperature too high
Action: prepare a fresh tray of seedlings but move to a cooler position as soon as they germinate

Problem: seedlings not receiving enough light
Action: move seedlings to a windowsill or into a more open position in the greenhouse

Sowing fine seed

As fine seeds won't need much space, a 9 cm (3½ in) pot or half tray may be big enough. Fill it to the rim with fine compost, tap it firmly then either water it from overhead or by standing the pot or tray in water until the compost is moist throughout. Check that the compost level is close to the rim.

Gently tap the seeds onto the compost surface. As dark seeds can be hidden against dark compost, they can be mixed with a pinch of dry, fine sand beforehand to help with even sowing.

Cover seeds with a fine dusting of sieved compost or a layer of fine vermiculite which allows light to reach the seeds but still retains moisture. Cover the tray or pot to retain moisture and place in a well lit position out of direct sunlight. Check that the compost remains moist, using a very fine spray to water when necessary. Very fine seedlings will emerge after several days.

Sowing seeds in modules

This is a useful method for larger seeds that need more space to develop and avoids the root disturbance of pricking out. Use a multi-purpose compost with high nutrient levels to support seedlings until they are planted out.

If using a flexible module insert, place it into a seed tray for stability. Overfill each cell with compost, tap the tray to allow the compost to settle and then remove the excess with a straight edge. Make a shallow hole in the compost with a dibber, so that the seed will sit at the correct depth. Sow either one or two seeds into each cell with the aim of removing one seedling if both seeds germinate. A quick tip is to gently rub the compost over the seed, but you can cover the seed with extra compost or vermiculite if you prefer. Water the compost to settle the seeds and then cover as before.

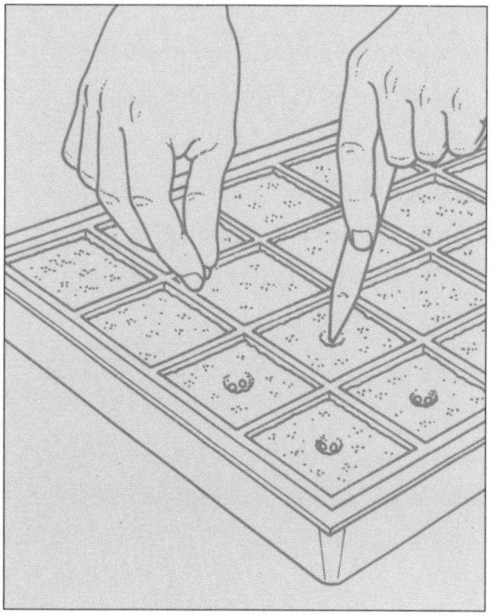

Sow larger seeds into modules

Special techniques

SOWING LARGE SEEDS

When quick-maturing plants have large seeds, sow two together in individual 9 cm (3½ in) pots. Use multi-purpose compost so the seedlings can germinate and grow on in the same pots until they are ready to be planted out. Remember to remove one seedling if both of the seeds germinate.

SOWING SLOW SEEDS

Some tree and shrub seeds need several weeks of low temperatures to trigger germination and are then slow to grow on. Sow as normal but cover the compost with grit to prevent algal growth on the surface, and be prepared to remove weed seedlings while waiting for germination to occur.

SEEDS THAT REQUIRE DARK

Some seeds won't germinate if exposed to light. In natural conditions, if they are sitting in deeper soil they are less likely to dry out so this mechanism helps with survival in changing moisture conditions. After covering the seeds with glass, clingfilm or a plastic lid, cover again with several sheets of newspaper to shut out most of the light.

SEEDS THAT REQUIRE LIGHT

Often very small seeds will not germinate well if they are planted too deep in the compost. Fine seeds can be covered with a thin layer of fine grade vermiculite rather than a dusting of compost as this allows the light to reach the seed while still preventing it from drying out.

SEED COLLECTION

Collecting seeds from plants to sow again the following year is an age-old practise which, however many times it is done, still holds a sense of personal achievement.

Plants need to be observed through the growing season to make sure that flowers have produced fruit. These need to be checked at regular intervals to see how the appearance changes as the fruit matures and with it the seeds inside. If the plant has plenty of flowers on it, some might mature earlier than others. If you can, allow some fruit or seed cases to mature and observe how the seed is shed so that you can make plans on how to collect it. With annuals, the length of time between flowering and seed dispersal will probably be quite quick but with perennials seed dispersal might occur months after flowering. Some vegetables and herbs are grown and harvested prior to flowering, so a few plants must be left in the ground and allowed to flower for seed collection. Once collected, the seed could be sown immediately if conditions are right but it is often stored until the following year.

Why collect seeds?

Where plants are hardy and quick to grow, their seeds can be allowed to fall to the ground in the hope that they will germinate the following year. Pot marigolds (*Calendula*), *Verbena bonariensis* and love-in-a-mist (*Nigella*) do this very successfully. However, over the winter and spring seeds will be lost to pests, rotting and possible soil disturbance, so collecting seed gives greater control.

LIMITATIONS

Growing plants from collected seed will usually bring great success but the seedlings will often show a slight variability from the parent plant. In many cases this goes unnoticed but in some plants, there can be problems with the quality of the seedlings.

Some cultivars may have lost crucial parts of their flower structure in the breeding process and may be sterile so unable to produce seed for collection.

Where flowers are cross-pollinated, pollen is transferred from another flowering plant of the same species growing close by. This means that the seeds could contain DNA from both parent plants, so that the resulting seedling plants won't necessarily all be identical to the parent from which the seed was collected.

Where a cultivar is a selected form of the species, the offspring from seed will not necessarily exhibit identical characteristics.

Seeds collected from the flowers of F1 hybrids (usually a few selected bedding plants or vegetables) will not show the vigour and uniformity of the parents.

Collection techniques

DRY SEED CASES

On some plants, the fruit containing the seeds dries and turns brown but continues to hold the seeds inside. Choose a dry day to pick the seed cases off the plant just as they might start to fall open. Hollyhocks, sweet peas, alliums and beans show this habit.

DRY SEED CASES THAT SPLIT OPEN

In many plants, the seed case dries and then splits open to release the seeds onto the soil. Poppies, aquilegias and hellebores show this habit. Remove seed heads from the plant as they dry out, or tie a paper bag over a chosen seed head before it opens and remove when the seed has fallen into it. Often the seed cases are upturned so attempt to be on hand soon after the seed case opens to tip seeds into a bag or envelope.

EXPLOSIVE SEED CASES

The seed case dries out and splits to forcibly expel the seeds away from the parent plant. The seeds can be caught by tying a paper bag over the seed head before the crucial moment arrives.

FLESHY FRUITS

Fleshy fruits and berries should be harvested when they are fully ripe as the flesh softens. The seeds can then be removed and cleaned.

Cleaning seeds

Seeds need to be dried and preferably cleaned of any plant debris to reduce spoilage from fungal diseases. Seeds are often heavier than chaff, so the latter can be blown away.

Collect seed cases and remove the ripe seed for storage

Seeds that are held inside fleshy fruits can be extracted by mashing the fruit then placing in a sieve under running water to wash off the flesh. Eventually only the seeds will remain and these can then be air-dried on a plate before storage.

Seed storage

To stop deterioration, most seeds need to be stored in cool, dark and dry conditions. When they are completely dry, store them in individual packages or containers such as envelopes, plastic camera film pots or glass jars and label each with the plant name and seed collection date. Put any seeds stored in paper into a watertight sealed container. Store dry seeds in the freezer, refrigerator or a cool, dark cupboard at a constant temperature.

SEED DORMANCY

Not all seed can be simply collected, stored and sown to grow into young plants. In nature, there are many situations where germinating seeds find it tough to survive. The moment when seeds fall to the ground may be ideal for germination in terms of temperature and soil conditions, but the young plants might fail to grow if the ensuing conditions become inhospitable. Nature overcomes this possibility by conferring dormancy on seeds so that they can only germinate when conditions are set to remain favourable for the developing plants.

Most commercial seeds from a packet will have been pretreated to overcome these problems, but collected seed may need special treatment to overcome dormancy and aid germination.

Scarification

A hard seed coat offers protection to a seed over winter as it prevents it germinating while it sits in the soil. By the spring the coat has been slowly broken down by rain and the abrasive quality of soil particles. Water permeates the seed coat in the spring, hydrates the seed and allows germination to progress.

To replicate this action, the seed coat needs to be slightly damaged. Only a few plants require this treatment, including sweet peas (*Lathyrus odoratus*) and species of morning glory (*Ipomoea*). The seed coats can be nicked one by one using a sharp knife but a safer method is to put the seeds into a jam jar containing sandpaper and shake vigorously for several minutes. Sow seed as normal.

PLANTS THAT REQUIRE SCARIFICATION

Alcea rosea	hollyhock
Brugmansia	angel's trumpet
Canna x generalis	canna
Ipomoea	morning glory
Lathyrus odoratus	sweet pea

Stratification

An ideal time for germination is in spring, after the freezing temperatures of winter. Many plants from colder climates delay seed germination until a period of cold has been endured. Seeds would naturally sit in cold wet soil over winter, so if saved seed is artificially exposed to a period of moist chill this should aid germination. There are two different methods.

- **Natural chill** Collect seeds or berries in autumn, sow into compost and cover with grit to deter pest damage. Place outside in a protected but unheated position such as a cold frame. The seeds must be exposed to approximately three weeks of temperatures below 0°C (37°F) during the winter period to trigger germination. In spring, seedlings will appear that can be pricked out and eventually potted on. Many trees and conifers respond to the fluctuating temperatures of winter to trigger germination so this method, though slow, does give reliable results.

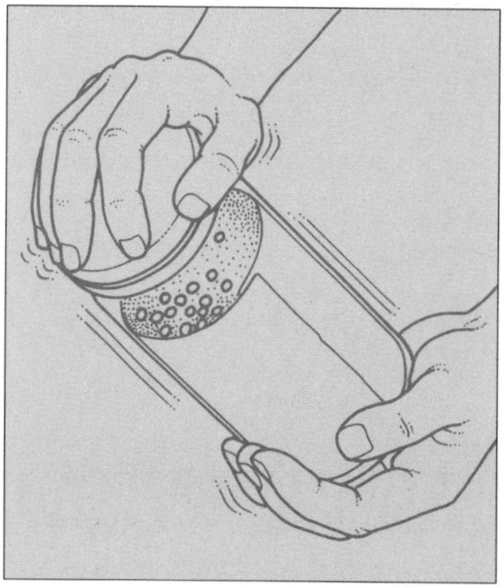

Breaking dormancy by scarification

PLANTS THAT REQUIRE STRATIFICATION

Aconitum	monkshood
Antirrhinum majus	snapdragon
Aquilegia	columbine
Clematis	clematis
Conifers	conifers
Helleborus	hellebore

- **Artificial chill** Collect seeds, mix with moist but not wet compost or vermiculite, place in a bag, jar or any suitable airtight container and mark with the date. Store in a refrigerator for a minimum of three weeks to simulate chilling. Check the seeds regularly thereafter for signs of germination. When about a third of the seeds have produced young embryonic roots, they can all be sown carefully onto trays or pots of compost and covered lightly.

Soaking

Some plants will delay germination until there is enough moisture in the soil for continued growth. The hard seed coat takes time to break down in the moist environment and allow water to permeate the seed. There may also be cases where germination is delayed by a coating of a chemical inhibitor on the seed coat. This is soluble and will be washed away by rainwater, but only very slowly, thereby delaying germination until conditions are more favourable. Both situations can be improved by soaking the seed.

Place the seeds in a bowl and cover with lukewarm water. The seeds should start to swell after several hours, so leaving them overnight is often enough. Strain off the water and sow them immediately. If they are left in the water for too long after swelling, the seeds are liable to rot. If they don't swell after 48 hours, the seeds may require scarification to speed the process.

Soak seeds in warm water before sowing

PLANTS THAT REQUIRE SOAKING

Armeria	thrift, sea pink
Canna (scarify before soaking)	canna
Euphorbia (stratify before soaking)	spurge
Hemerocallis	daylily
Hibiscus	hibiscus
Lathyrus odoratus	sweet pea

GROWING PLANTS FROM CUTTINGS

A cutting is made when part of a plant is removed and encouraged to grow roots or shoots so that it forms an independent plant. Cuttings are most often taken from the stem of a plant, but sections of root can be encouraged to shoot and for some plants leaf cuttings can be successful.

Cuttings need to be prepared using a clean, sharp blade – usually a knife or secateurs – to reduce the possibility of damage to and infection of the cut surface. The cuttings are then placed into a rooting medium, often based on compost mixed with other materials to help with drainage or aeration and create the ideal conditions for growth.

In all but a few cases, cuttings need to be placed in carefully controlled conditions immediately after preparation, until they start to produce new shoots and roots and become a plant in their own right. This may involve a raised temperature to promote rooting and a humid environment to prevent the cuttings losing too much water from their leaves and drying out. These conditions can be provided quite simply by covering the cuttings with a plastic bag and placing them on a windowsill, or by using more sophisticated propagation equipment (see page 129).

The advantages of cuttings

A cutting will grow to be identical to the part of the parent plant from which it was taken. If a plant shows an uncharacteristic but interesting leaf marking, plants grown from stem cuttings should hopefully retain this quality. However, if seed was collected from this plant, the seedlings would be less likely to show the marking in the foliage. One exception where the cutting is not identical is in variegated plants. A stem cutting will retain the variegation but a root cutting taken of a variegated plant will have plain green leaves.

What to take

Cuttings can be taken from many perennials as well as shrubs, trees and climbers. The plants can be hardy outdoor ornamentals, fruit-bearing plants, plants bought for summer patio containers or indoor plants.

The age of the cutting material can affect the rate of success. Very young, soft material can be quick to root but difficult to keep from rotting in humid conditions whereas more woody material is easy to handle but slow to root, so vulnerable to drying out over a long period. Usually successful cuttings are made using new growth that is less than one year old when that part of the plant is still growing quite quickly.

A range of plant parts can be used successfully to form cuttings, such as shoot tips, stems or leaves, but the success of the cutting type can depend greatly on the individual plant itself. It is through experience that propagators have found which part of the plant gives the greatest chance for success in individual varieties.

Cutting a shoot tip

As the success rate is variable, always take more cuttings than you initially require as plants. If the success rate is only 50 per cent and you want three plants, then take at least six cuttings to allow for losses. If they all succeed, the extras can be given to friends, but if they all fail, don't be disheartened – just try again. It might also be worth trying a different technique or adjusting the rooting environment.

Root development in cuttings

There are regions of every plant where growth is taking place, most notably in the tips of shoots and roots, in leaves as they grow larger and in the stems and trunks. Plants grow when cells in these growing regions divide into two over and over again, so increasing their numbers. Similarly, when a plant is damaged in some way, the living plant cells will produce large numbers of new cells to try and repair the damage. In propagation, when a stem is cut, cells in the stem start to divide rapidly to seal the wound. This can be seen as an area of swollen brown growth called a callus. In root and leaf cuttings this may not be so visible but the process is the same. Chemicals in the

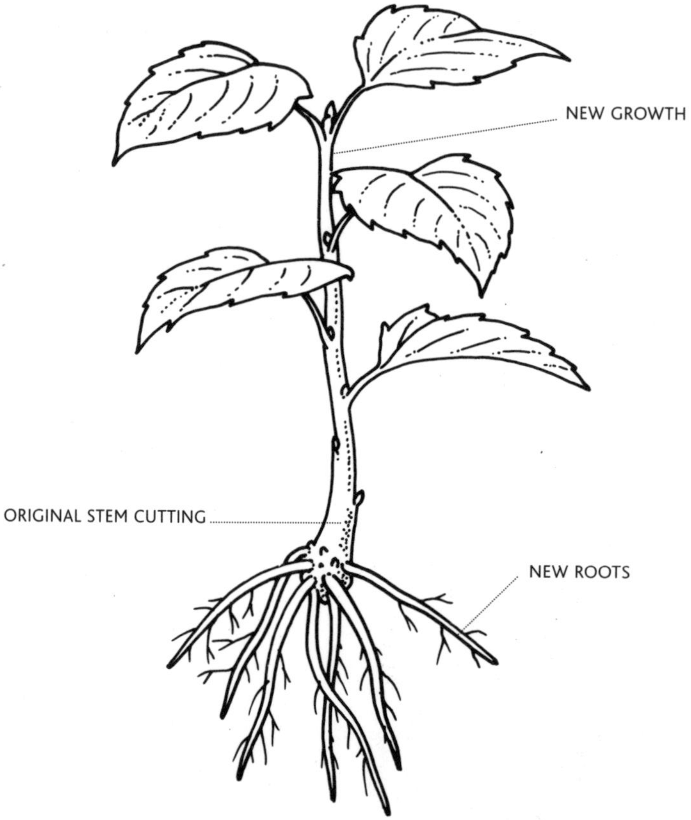

Root and shoot growth show when a cutting has been successful

plant cells can then trigger a mechanism whereby these cells start to change their function to become part of the mix of different cells that make plant roots and shoots.

Regardless of whether the cutting was originally from leaf, stem or root, the aim is to provide conditions for new roots, leaves and stems to grow to produce independent plants.

The process of cell division requires a food source for fuel and this is usually what is initially contained in the cutting or what can be made if the cutting material has leaves attached. The speed of cell division can increase as the temperature increases, so a warm environment will always aid cuttings.

The cells will cease to divide should the plant material dry out. As large amounts of water are lost through the leaves, cuttings with leaves attached need to be kept in more humid conditions than those without leaves.

Simple cuttings

If you have never taken a cutting before and are unsure where to begin, try with cuttings that you can place on a windowsill. Start by picking off the tips of stems from houseplants like the wandering jew (*Tradescantia*), or the baby plantlets on the spider plant (*Chlorophytum*). Place the stem tips or plantlets with their bases in a jar of water. When they grow new roots, pot them on into fresh houseplant compost. This method will only work for a few plants, so once you have had a go, do try taking stem cuttings of outdoor plants in summer. Follow the instructions for collecting and trimming them and then keep an eye on them as they sit on the windowsill covered with a plastic bag. There is nothing better than growing more plants for free, so if they don't root just have another go.

EQUIPMENT FOR TAKING CUTTINGS

Much of the equipment required for taking cuttings is the same equipment used for growing seeds, but it may be used in a slightly different way.

- **Secateurs** These are required for removing cutting material from the parent plant and can be used to prepare woody cuttings. Ensure that they are clean and sharp.
- **Sharp knife or blade** A straight-bladed knife is used to trim cuttings. A blade that folds away into a wooden or plastic handle is safer. Ensure the blade is clean and sharp. A scalpel or craft knife with disposable blades is useful for cutting very soft stems.
- **Seed trays** These are good for housing large numbers of small cuttings. The shallow depth of compost brings the base of cuttings into close contact with the heat source (if you are using bottom heat to aid rooting). Drainage holes stop cuttings from rotting off in wet compost. Available in standard, half and quarter seed tray sizes.

- **Modules** These are available as plastic inserts of various sizes that sit in a seed tray and divide it into individual plugs of soil to house individual cuttings. Also available as large stand-alone trays. They produce individual root systems that are less prone to damage when potted on.
- **Pots** Good for holding just a few cuttings or individual large cuttings. The extra depth suits a larger root system.
- **Pot covers** Used to cover the cuttings and maintain a humid environment to reduce water loss while cuttings are forming roots.
- **Propagator** A moulded tray with a moulded cover into which one or several seed trays or pots can be placed. The tray collects drainage water from the compost and the tight cover will retain moisture and create a slight lift in temperature that can speed rooting. Electric heated propagators are also available (see page 25).
- **Dibber** Used to dig down under the roots when cuttings are ready to be potted individually. A pencil or stick will do.
- **Labels** These can be bought or made but they need to be waterproof.
- **Pen/pencil** A special waterproof pen is ideal, but a pencil will also do.
- **Watering can** Fit a fine rose so the water is delivered as a fine spray, or use a water mister as an alternative.

COVERING CUTTINGS

PLASTIC BAG • A small bag can be tightly secured around the pot. Small pots can be placed individually in large bags, closed and secured at the top. Small sticks can be used to support the plastic above the cuttings. The bags will need to be ventilated and re-inflated every few days.

MOULDED CLEAR PLASTIC • Rigid plastic covers are available to cover seed trays, half trays or pots. Choose taller covers to allow space for larger cuttings.

FLEECE • A useful cover for cuttings of plants suited to lower levels of humidity. It can also provide shading.

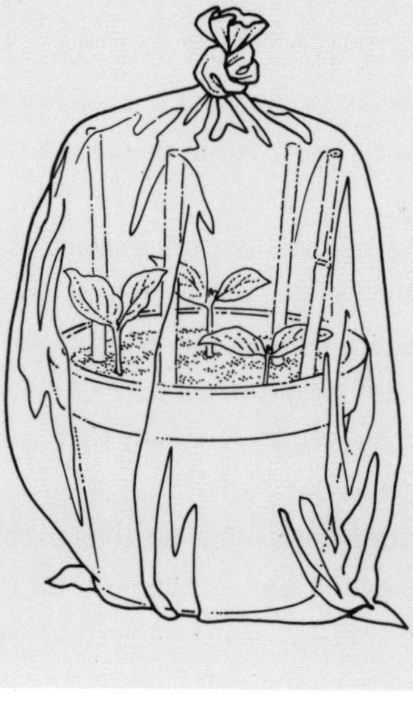

Choosing compost

As soon as a cutting is made, it is vulnerable to drying out. The cutting must be quickly inserted into a rooting medium that will hold water and keep the cut surface continually moist. Some plants grow in drier soils than others, so the cuttings of these plants might prefer similar conditions.

- A compost used for cuttings needs to be water retentive, but with drainage so that it is also well aerated to encourage healthy root growth.
- It should be firm enough to support the heavier stems of larger cuttings.
- It should be sterile so that the cuttings are not weakened by tiny pests, diseases or copious weed seedlings.

Composts are prepared using a variety of materials and to different qualities so that they can be used to suit different purposes. See pages 26–27 for details of the composts and different materials available.

OTHER COMPONENTS

Many successful propagators develop their own cuttings compost based on their successes and the soil requirements of the plant. You may wish to try the following components:

- **Fine grit or coarse sand** This creates a more open texture to a compost, adding drainage for alpine and succulent cuttings. It also adds stability for larger cuttings.
- **Perlite** This is a white, sterile and inert material formed from expanded volcanic rock granules. It looks like polystyrene balls, but is crunchy. It has a light open texture but retains water while allowing the excess to drain freely. It is useful to lighten and aerate a compost. Try to wet the perlite before adding to the compost as it is very dusty and easily inhaled.
- **Vermiculite** This is a pale brown expanded mica. It can be used as an additive instead of perlite but holds more water and less air. It still helps with drainage and aeration of the compost.

Magnolia cuttings in a tray of perlite

STEM CUTTINGS EXPLAINED

To make a stem cutting a section of plant stem is removed, trimmed to size with a sharp knife, inserted into moist compost and placed in a light, warm position to encourage rooting.

The cutting will need a supply of food to grow new roots and this will come from what is already stored in the stem or from what is made in the leaves during daylight hours by the process of photosynthesis. Until the cutting has produced roots of its own it is very vulnerable to drying out as it cannot take in further water, but will continue to lose vital supplies through its leaves. Often, a few leaves are removed from the cutting to reduce water loss, but not so many as to compromise food manufacture. In general, fresh cuttings need to be placed in a bright position so that photosynthesis can continue, but also in a moist and possibly enclosed environment to reduce water loss from the leaves.

Age of cutting material

When taking cuttings from different plants at different times of year, you will encounter plants at different stages of growth. New, soft shoots are normally produced during spring, although the time of shoot emergence is earlier for some plants than for others. The new shoots will be soft and delicate and are very vulnerable to drying out if they are detached from the parent plant at this time. Cuttings taken at this time are called softwood cuttings.

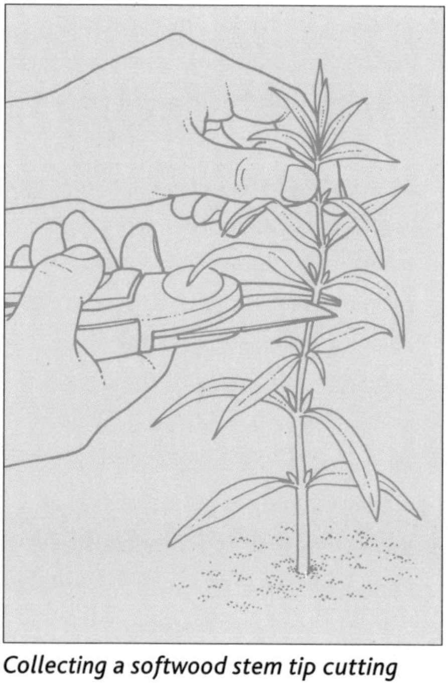

Collecting a softwood stem tip cutting

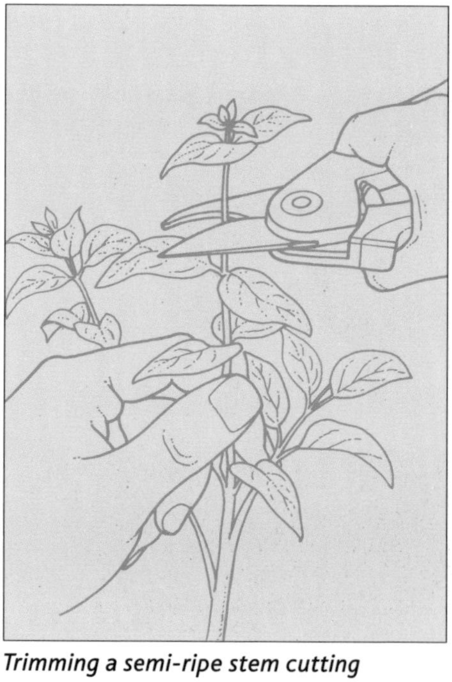

Trimming a semi-ripe stem cutting

Slowly, as the season progresses, new shoots on a woody stemmed plant toughen up and start to show a slight stiffness as the first layers of woodiness begin to develop. Cuttings taken at this stage are called semi-ripe cuttings.

By the end of the growing season this woodiness will have developed further so that the stems are less flexible with signs of the young bark developing. Cuttings taken at the end of the growing season into winter are called hardwood cuttings.

In the second year of growth, these stems become woodier still and less able to root as cuttings, but they will in turn produce new shoots of younger growth that will itself make good cutting material.

Types of cutting material

It has been found that a variety of stem cuttings can be taken from a plant, depending on its growth habit. Some plants root readily from cuttings of any type; others have been found to only root successfully if the cutting is taken in a certain way.

STEM TIP CUTTINGS

This type of cutting is taken from young growth at the tip of a shoot. It can be the tip of any stem less than one year old. It is usually the easiest method of taking cuttings with a good chance of success. If the very tip of the cutting is too soft, it can be removed to reduce the chance of it rotting in a humid environment.

Some plants may produce many short side shoots that are quite weak and soft. These can be trimmed in such a way as to increase the chances of successful rooting (see page 47).

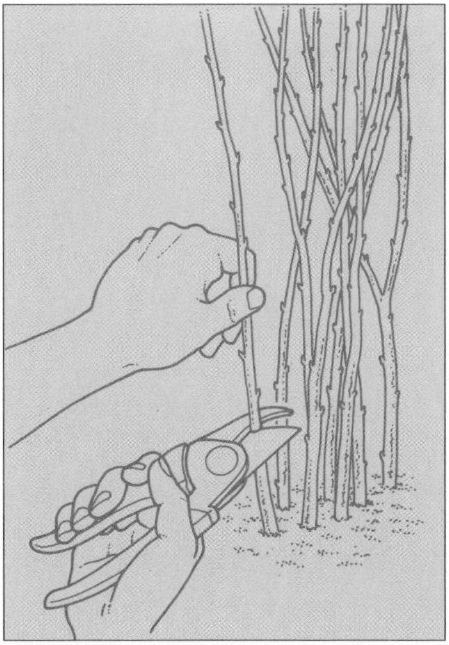

Taking woody stems for hardwood cuttings

STEM CUTTINGS

Some plants root so well from cuttings that not only will the stem tip root easily, but short sections down the same stem can also be taken and rooted. Make the first cut across the stem just above a leaf node, then make a lower cut across the stem below 2–3 sets of leaves. Continue working down the stem, cutting it into short lengths each with 2–3 sets of leaves. Use only the new growth, as stem cuttings from the older wood of previous years will be less successful.

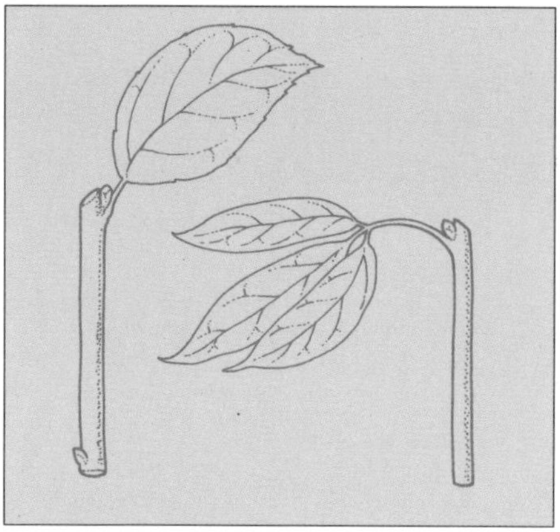

Leaf bud cuttings

LEAF BUD CUTTINGS

These are a variation on stem cuttings, but use very little plant material. A short section of stem is taken and trimmed to just above a leaf bud as it sits between the main stem and the leaf joint. Trim the stem to a few centimetres below the bud but above the next leaf on the stem.

Cutting from the parent plant.

When taking cutting material, think about the effect it will have on the appearance and subsequent growth of the parent plant. If the plant has been bought specifically for propagation, this is of no importance. However, if the plant is in the garden, cut the stems at a leaf joint as if pruning. This avoids short stem snags that often die back. Once the cutting material has been collected, it may need further trimming to make the correct cut.

Trimming a cutting

Leaves may be arranged on a stem in pairs, or singly on alternate sides of the stem. At the point of attachment, the stem is often slightly swollen. This area is called a leaf node. At each leaf node, there is a bud between the leaf and the stem. This bud has the ability to develop into a new stem when conditions are correct. When plants root easily from cuttings, it doesn't matter where the cut in the stem is made. For most plants, however, the chance of rooting is increased if the stem is trimmed at a leaf node.

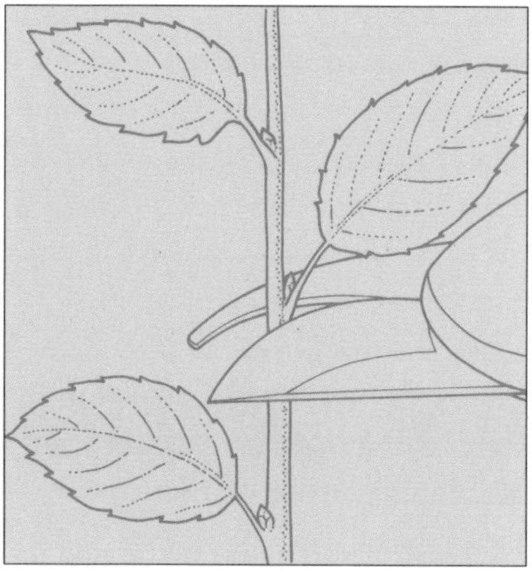

Nodal cuttings are trimmed at the leaf joint

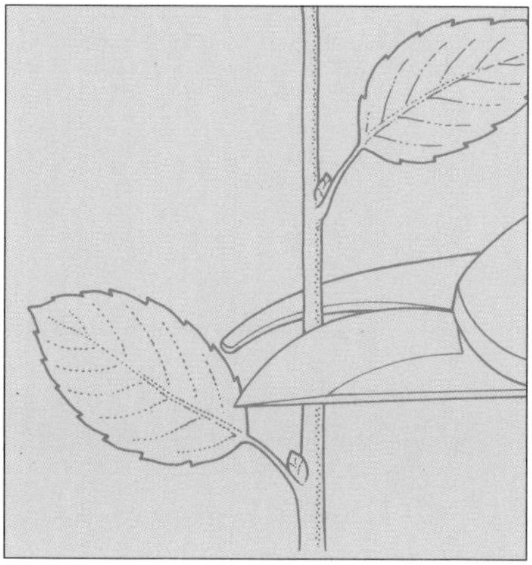

An internodal cutting (between leaf joints)

NODAL CUTTINGS

The cut is made across the plant stem just below a leaf node where there is slight swelling. Nodal cuttings are good for plants with hollow stems as they are less likely to rot off in the compost because the stem is usually sealed at the node.

INTERNODAL CUTTINGS

The cut is made across the stem about half way between the nodes. This type of trimming is used on both stem tip and stem cuttings.

BASAL CUTTINGS

These are a refinement on stem tip cuttings. If soft growth is used in spring, the stems can rot easily at the cutting base. To avoid this, take basal cuttings. The cut is made at the point where a new side shoot joins the older stem. Be sure to include some of the firmer growth of the older wood to reduce the chance of rotting. This method can be used where side shoots are still short, but when the cutting material is collected the older stem from the previous season needs to be included.

HEEL CUTTINGS

These follow a similar principle to basal cuttings. The short side shoot is removed by pulling it away from the older stem to include some of the stem as a 'tail' to the cutting. This slightly older wood at the base reduces the potential for rotting. Also, the resulting increase in exposed stem tissue improves the chances of root formation.

MALLET CUTTINGS

These go one step further in incorporating old wood at the base of the cutting. In this case, the side shoot remains attached to the older stem. The stem is trimmed above and below where the shoot sits. This is especially useful for plants where the young shoots have hollow or soft pithy centres and would readily rot in moist compost.

Basal cutting

Heel cutting

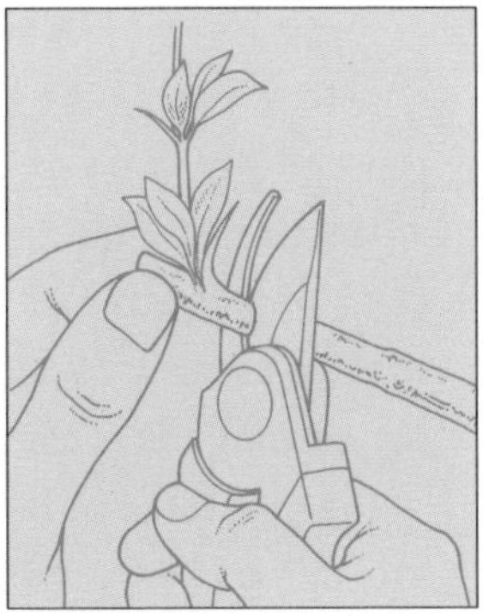

Mallet cutting

Root development in stem cuttings

In the plant stem there are areas of cells that have the ability to divide into two over and over again. This results in an increase in stem girth. These areas of cells form the cambium. When a stem is cut, if the plant cells are kept hydrated, then cambium cells in the stem start to divide rapidly to seal the wound. This can be seen as an area of swollen brown growth called a callus. Chemicals in the plant cells can then trigger a mechanism whereby these cells start to change their function to become part of the mix of different cells that make plant roots. Once roots have formed the cutting will stay hydrated and hopefully go on to produce leaves.

Increasing the chances of rooting

- **Shoot selection** Always select healthy growth, as any condition that puts the plant under stress will divert energy from root production. Similarly, select non-flowering stems so that all the effort goes to root production rather than flowers. If only flowering shoots are available, pinch out the flowers and any flower buds during the rooting process.
- **Wounding** In woody stems that are beginning to harden at the end of the summer, the outer layer of bark is already forming. Any new roots will originate from the cambium underneath the bark. If the bark layer is physically removed the chance of root emergence should increase. Semi-ripe cuttings are often 'wounded' to improve rooting by removing a thin sliver of bark from the base of the cutting. Making a heel cutting also exposes the cambium cells.
- **Rooting hormone** Plants manufacture a variety of chemicals to control their function. Chemicals are produced at the shoot tips to promote cell division. These chemicals are known collectively as auxins (rooting hormones) and their presence promotes rooting in stem cuttings. Different plants produce different levels of auxins, and this contributes to the ease at which they root from cuttings. It is also known that levels of auxins are higher at leaf nodes, which is why it is a good idea to trim cuttings just below a node.

  Preparations of rooting hormone are available that contain synthetic versions of naturally occurring auxins. There are also natural plant extracts containing concentrated levels of natural plant auxins. Both types of preparation aim to increase the chance and rate of successful rooting by their application to the cut stem. To apply, transfer a small amount of the rooting hormone to another container when in use and discard the unused portion when you have finished. This avoids plant sap entering the pot and possibly allowing the transfer of disease.

  Dip only the exposed stem in the rooting hormone. If it is a powder, tap off the excess. Too much rooting hormone can prevent cuttings from rooting. These preparations have a short shelf life so buy fresh stock every year.

Look for signs of rooting before potting on

Monitoring progress

Callus formation can be a critical time in the process of rooting, so avoid exposing the cut ends of the cuttings at this stage. If you are not sure if a cutting has rooted, pulling it out of the compost at the critical time can prevent roots developing. Therefore, it is best not to disturb cuttings once inserted and to look for other signs that roots may have developed.

- Be patient and don't expect rooting to take place overnight.
- Look for signs of leaf wilt or leaf fall. Unless it is autumn, leaf fall may well indicate that the cutting has failed.
- Look for buds opening to expose new leaves. This doesn't guarantee rooting but the cutting is still alive and active. Once these extend to form shoots, then rooting is very likely to have occurred.
- Lift up the tray or pot and look for signs of root growth extending out through the drainage holes.
- Very gently pull at the cutting to see if it resists due to the presence of roots acting as anchorage. Be careful not to pull too hard or you might damage a delicate and hard-earned root system.

SOFTWOOD CUTTINGS

Softwood cuttings are usually taken in the spring or early summer from young shoots. At this stage of growth the stems are soft and pliable with no woodiness and the leaves are also very soft. These shoots tend to flop and dry out quickly once they are removed from the plant, so they need to be placed in a humid environment while roots develop. As the plant is growing fast, roots will develop quickly, but the soft growth is prone to rotting in a humid atmosphere. For success with softwood cuttings the trick is to achieve rooting before rotting.

Which plants to use

Softwood cuttings can be taken from trees, shrubs and climbers as new shoots develop on established stems over the spring months. It is easier to identify new material on deciduous plants as any green growth that appears in spring will be new wood. On evergreens, the new growth will be the soft tips and side shoots on existing stems.

Other candidates for softwood cuttings include the new shoots of herbaceous perennials if there is good leaf growth, the new growth of tender perennials used for patio tubs, and the soft shoots of many houseplants.

Creating material for cuttings

No preparation is needed if only a few cuttings are required from a plant. If you want to collect a large number of shoots from trees or shrubs, however, prune the stem tips in the previous season to promote plenty of new growth the following year.

Selecting material

As softwood cuttings wilt easily, the ideal time for collection is early in the day. Select only the stems that are healthy and are growing true to type. Avoid damaged and distorted growth. Vigorous upright shoots with the leaf nodes more widely spaced apart tend not to root so readily, so look for material that is growing less vigorously. Avoid stems where flower buds are developing, unless there is no other suitable material.

Use sharp secateurs to remove stems from selected plants. When taking material for cuttings, always cut the stem just above a leaf node to leave the plant looking good with no stem snags that can die back later. Place the cutting material in a plastic bag to prevent moisture loss. They can be stored in a sealed plastic bag in the refrigerator for several hours if required.

Preparing the container

Smaller cuttings will suit trays or modules, larger cuttings are better placed in deeper compost in a pot. Different plants root over different periods of time, so avoid putting cuttings of different plants in the same container as it can cause problems when trying to pot them up. Before taking the cuttings, fill seed trays or pots with the selected compost mixture so the cuttings can be potted up without delay. Cuttings of silver-leaved and drought-tolerant plants may prefer a compost with good drainage (see page 43).

Preparing the cuttings

Remove the cuttings from the plastic bag a few at a time. Trim the cuttings by placing them on a hard surface and cutting across below a leaf node using a sharp-bladed knife. Cuttings should be about 7.5–10 cm (3–4 in) long.

Remove the leaves from the lower half of the stem as they will rot in the compost and possibly cause the stem to rot. Use a knife to trim off the leaves close to the stem. Alternatively, use finger and thumb nails to pinch off the leaves. Leave at least two leaves on the stem, more if the leaves are very small. A good leaf area is needed to produce food to fuel the new root growth. Large leaves can be trimmed in half to retain a good leaf area while at the same time reducing the amount of water lost through the leaves.

Remove the very tip of the cutting where the new leaves are just emerging from the bud. This will reduce the chance of rotting.

Dip the base of the stem into rooting hormone, then use a dibber to make a hole in the compost. Place the stem into the hole so that the lower leaf or leaves are resting just above the compost surface. Firm the compost around the stem of the cutting using the dibber.

Continue to insert cuttings so that the leaves just avoid touching. Not all cuttings may root so assume a third will fail and insert more than you need. Label the container with the plant name and date, then water the cuttings thoroughly using a fine spray from a watering can or hose.

Aftercare

Cuttings need to be kept moist and warm. A few cuttings in a pot can be sealed in a clear polythene bag. Short plant sticks will help support the bag over the cuttings. Alternatively, use clear plastic tray or pot covers.

Pots or trays can be placed on a warm windowsill, in a greenhouse or conservatory or in a heated propagator. As they are covered, the cuttings are unlikely to require extra water initially but check them daily and keep the compost moist but not saturated. Plastic bags may need to be re-ventilated if the sides collapse together. Remove any

Trim the cutting with a sharp knife

Remove lower leaves and place in the hole

cuttings if their leaves or the stem start to turn brown. After three or four weeks, start looking for signs of rooting (see page 49).

Potting on

Once rooted, cuttings can tolerate a cooler and less humid environment. Remove from bottom heat, start to ventilate propagators or slowly split open plastic bags over several days. After the cuttings have had a few days to acclimatize, they can be potted singly into fresh compost.

Part-fill 10 cm (4 in) pots with multipurpose compost. Use a dibber under the cutting to release its roots, then hold the cutting in the centre of the pot so that it sits at the same level as before. Gently fill the pot with more compost, then firm it carefully around the cutting. Label and water thoroughly. Return cuttings to their original positions to acclimatize after the root disturbance of potting.

After a few days, the cuttings can be moved to a cold frame or outside in a sheltered spot. As the young plants grow, they can be potted on to a larger pot and will be ready for planting out in the autumn or following spring, depending on garden conditions.

Greenwood cuttings

As spring proceeds, the new soft growth on woody plants starts to firm while the shoot is still growing at the tip. As the stem matures, the first fine layers of bark will start to develop, although often the change isn't visible. This material can be removed to make

WHAT CAN GO WRONG

LEAVES TURN BROWN, START TO ROT AND FALL OFF	LEAVES CURL UP, TURN BROWN AND FALL OFF
Problem: the environment is too humid **Action:** maintain a moist compost but don't overwater. Consider more ventilation **Problem:** the compost is too wet, causing stem rot **Action:** make a 60:40 mixture of compost with perlite or vermiculite to aid drainage and aeration	**Problem:** the cuttings have dried out **Action:** create a more humid environment by watering and using an airtight cover **SOME CUTTINGS FAIL TO ROOT** **Problem:** cuttings are too small **Action:** ensure cuttings are a good size **Problem:** unsuitable plant material was selected **Action:** ensure you take only new growth

PLANTS SUITABLE FOR SOFTWOOD CUTTINGS

Any young stem tips from trees or shrubs in spring or summer:

Amelanchier	snowy mespilus
Cornus alba	dogwood
Kerria japonica	kerria
Philadelphus	mock orange
Sambucus	elder
Spiraea	spiraea
Viburnum carlesii	viburnum
Weigela	weigela

Young stems from hardy perennials in spring:

Diascia	diascia
Salvia	sage
Sedum	ice plant

Stem tips from houseplants and tender perennials grown under cover in spring or summer:

Bougainvillea	bougainvillea
Ficus benjamina	weeping fig
Peperomia	peperomia
Tradescantia	wandering jew

Stem tips from patio plants:

Argyranthemum	margeurite
Fuchsia	fuchsia
Helichrysum petiolare	helichrysum
Solenostemon	coleus
Verbena x hybrida	verbena

greenwood cuttings. This slightly more mature material is taken at the end of spring and is easier to handle than softwood as it is less likely to wilt. Plants that can be successfully propagated by softwood cuttings (see page 49) usually root well as greenwoods and should be treated in the same way.

SEMI-RIPE CUTTINGS

Semi-ripe cuttings can be taken from midsummer to early autumn depending on the weather, the type of plant and where the cuttings are to be placed for rooting. If you can provide heat and protection as outdoor temperatures start to fall, cuttings can be taken later in the year.

These cuttings are taken from plants that are naturally woody when mature. Stems are selected from new growth that is still soft at the tips, but stiffer and less pliable lower down and may show the first signs of the brown bark developing. These shoots are tougher than softwood and so less likely to fail as cuttings. However, as growth slows down later in the year rooting takes longer, typically 6–8 weeks.

Semi-ripe cuttings are the easiest for beginners or those with little specialist equipment as they require less attention and provide good success rates.

Which plants to use

Semi-ripe cuttings can be taken from trees, shrubs and woody climbers as new shoots start to ripen later in the growing season.

Many patio plants are tender woody perennials, and their shoots will also start to ripen by late summer, making them ideal for semi-ripe cuttings.

Creating material for cuttings

No preparation is needed if only a few cuttings are required. If a large number of cuttings are required, prune shrubs all over in the previous summer to promote plenty of new shoots the following year.

Selecting material

Select only stems from plants that are healthy and with typical growth. Avoid damaged or distorted growth or where pests are evident. Select non-flowering stems where possible. If there is no other suitable material, remove the flowers or flower buds when preparing the cutting.

Use sharp secateurs to remove semi-ripe stems from selected plants. Always cut the stem just above a leaf node to avoid leaving stem snags on the plant. Place the cut material in a plastic bag to prevent water loss. Pot up straight away or store in a sealed plastic bag in the refrigerator for several hours if required.

Preparing the cuttings

Trim the cut shoots by placing them one at a time on a clean, smooth, hard surface such as a wall tile and cut using a sharp knife.

Cuttings can be prepared as nodal stem tips, basal cuttings or heel cuttings (see page 47) depending on the growth habit of the plant. Trim the cuttings to about 6–10 cm (2½–4 in) long and remove the leaves from the base of the stem using the knife or your finger and thumb nails. Leave the final cutting with at least two sets of leaves.

To promote root growth, wound the cutting by shaving off a thin slice of young bark from the lower 2.5 cm (1 in) of stem. The cut surface allows roots to emerge more easily.

Dip the base of each cutting into rooting hormone, then insert the cuttings into the prepared pots or modules so that the lower leaves come just above the compost surface. Label and date the pots, then water thoroughly using a fine spray from a watering can or hose.

The rooting environment

Semi-ripe cuttings can be placed in a variety of settings to root successfully. Easy-to-root hardy plant cuttings can be inserted into a patch of well-prepared soil in a border. Mix in some potting compost and water well. Keep them covered with a cloche and shade from strong sunlight.

If you have just a few cuttings, place three to a 10 cm (4 in) pot, cover with a clear polythene bag or pot cover and place in a warm, sheltered site outdoors or in a shaded cold frame.

For larger numbers, cuttings can be inserted into individual modules and placed in a propagator or on a heated bench in the greenhouse to speed up rooting.

Cuttings of tender perennials can be placed in a propagator or heated greenhouse to root. Keep in a well-lit, frost-free environment through the winter.

Aftercare

Check cuttings regularly and water the compost as required to keep it moist. Remove any fallen leaves. As autumn approaches the leaves will fall from deciduous stems, but leave cuttings in the compost as they might already have rooted.

If you are providing bottom heat to speed up rooting, remove from the heat once signs of successful rooting are apparent. As temperatures fall later in the year, leave cuttings in their original containers but ensure they are protected from extremes of weather in a bright position.

Potting on

Once the cuttings have started back into growth in spring, pot them on into individual pots of multi-purpose compost to accommodate their root systems. Pinch out the growing tips to make the plants bushier. If they are large enough, plant out at the end of summer, or pot on again and plant out as bigger plants the following spring. Rooted

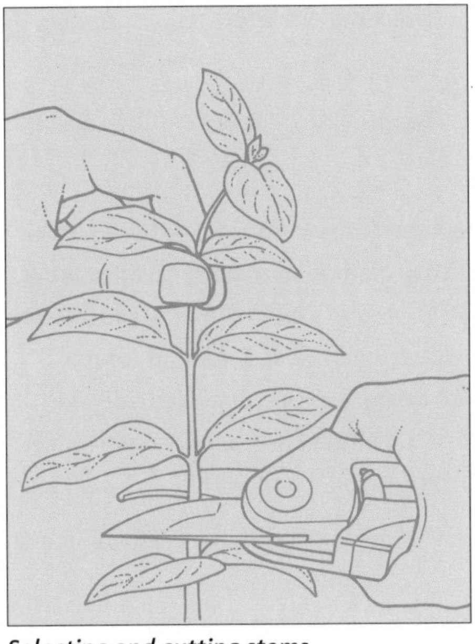

Selecting and cutting stems

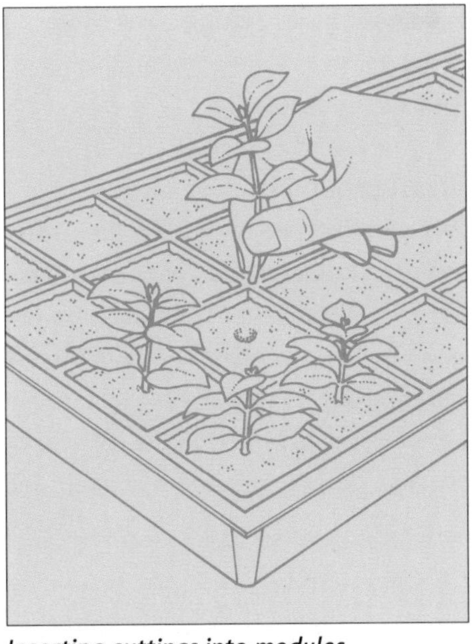

Inserting cuttings into modules

WHAT CAN GO WRONG

PLANTS FAIL TO ROOT

Problem: position is too cold
Action: try taking cuttings slightly earlier in the summer, or root in a warmer position

cuttings that have remained outside under a cloche can be hardened off and transplanted in late summer to their final positions.

Conifer cuttings

Cuttings of conifers can be taken in midsummer or autumn using semi-ripe wood. Most varieties will root successfully by this method although some, namely *Abies* and *Picea*, do well from softwood cuttings. When taking cuttings later in the year, take them with a heel, preferably from strong leading shoots so that the new plants take on the upright habit. Cuttings taken from horizontal shoots can grow into plants with a lax growth habit.

PLANTS SUITABLE FOR SEMI-RIPE CUTTINGS

Artemesia	wormwood
Aucuba japonica	spotted laurel
Buxus sempervirens	box
Callicarpa	beauty bush
Camellia	camellia
Ceanothus	Californian lilac
Cotoneaster	cotoneaster
Euonymus	spindle
Forsythia	forsythia
Hebe	hebe
Hydrangea	hydrangea
Lavandula	lavender
Lonicera	honeysuckle
Penstemon	penstemon
Pieris	pieris
Potentilla fructicosa	shrubby potentilla
Rosmarinus officinalis	rosemary
Viburnum	viburnum
Weigela	weigela

Dianthus pipings

This is a term used to describe the cuttings taken from some forms of Dianthus, notably border pinks, alpine pinks and carnations. It is an easy method of making cuttings using semi-ripe growth after flowering in summer. Look for strong shoots showing a rosette of leaves and gently pull at the base. The stem should easily break at a node to form a cutting about 7.5–10 cm (3–4 in) long, shorter for alpine varieties. Remove the lower pair of leaves and insert into a cuttings compost or a multipurpose compost with added drainage. Cover to prevent drying out, and the cuttings should root within 2–3 weeks.

BASAL CUTTINGS

This is a useful method for plants that produce very soft, often hollow stems in spring. It is used mainly for herbaceous perennials that grow from a woody stem system. As new shoots develop in spring, some are cut away and treated like softwood cuttings. They are removed at the point of attachment to the old stems, giving a slightly firmer base which is less likely to rot. Some plants develop hollow stems as the shoots extend, but the stem base is often still solid and less likely to rot, so basal cuttings will be the best method to choose.

Which plants to use

This method is suitable for herbaceous perennials where the new shoots often arise from a single central stem. It is particularly useful when the parent plants are difficult to lift for division, or dislike the root disturbance that division brings. The new shoots of dahlias, for example, offer good cutting material. Remember not to take too many basal cuttings or the plant may perform poorly in following summer.

Creating material for cuttings

No preparation is required for hardy plants in borders, except to trim back the old dead stems in spring to expose the new shoots. Cuttings can be taken earlier if plants are lifted and moved to a warmer protected environment to stimulate early growth. Dahlias and other tender subjects can be potted up and placed in a heated greenhouse in early spring to encourage shoots to develop.

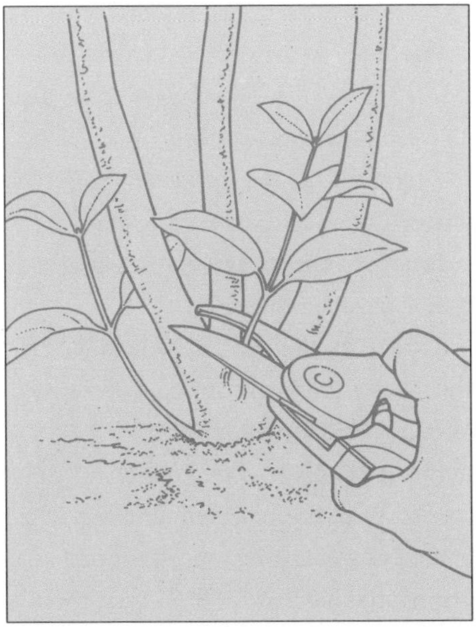

Removing a shoot close to the main stem

Selecting material

Select new shoots when they are 7.5–10 cm (3–4 in) long from the point where they are attached to the old stem. The stem must be clearly extending with nodes visible.

Cut the shoots from the main plant at the point of attachment to the old stem using secateurs or a sharp knife. If the shoot appears to be attached below soil or compost level, scrape it away to expose the base of the shoot and make the cut there. Place the cuttings in a plastic bag to prevent wilting if there is any delay before potting up.

Take basal cuttings of lupins in early spring

PLANTS SUITABLE FOR BASAL CUTTINGS

Achillea	yarrow
Aster	michaelmas daisy
Chrysanthemum	chrysanthemum
Dahlia	dahlia
Delphinium	delphinium
Gaura lindheimeri	butterfly plant
Geranium macrorrhizum, G. sanguineum	cranesbill
Knautia macedonica	knautia
Lupinus	lupin
Salvia (herbaceous)	salvia
Veronica	speedwell

WHAT CAN GO WRONG

Basal cuttings can encounter all the problems that can be experienced with softwood cuttings (see page 49).

Preparing the cuttings

Prepare a few cuttings at a time. Leave the bases of the cuttings untrimmed but pinch or cut off the lower leaves so there is 2.5–5 cm (1–2 in) of clear stem for insertion into the compost. At least two pairs of leaves should remain to fuel root growth.

Dip the bases of the cuttings in rooting hormone then use a dibber to make a hole in the compost. Insert the stems so that the lower leaves come just above the compost surface. Gently firm the compost around the stems using the dibber. Continue to insert prepared cuttings so that the leaves just avoid touching each other.

Label with the plant name and date, then water thoroughly using a fine spray from a watering can or hose. Immediately cover with a plastic bag or tray cover to prevent them drying out. The cuttings must be kept moist and warm, at about 15°C (59°F). Treat them as for softwood cuttings (see page 49).

LEAF BUD CUTTINGS

Leaf bud cuttings are a variation on softwood or semi-ripe cuttings, due to the way the stem is cut. These cuttings are very economical with material as the complete cutting consists of only a short piece of stem, a leaf and the bud contained in the leaf apex. New growth will emerge from the leaf bud rather than the tip of the cutting. This technique allows for several cuttings to be created from a single stem, so long as the material is still less than a year old. Cuttings can be taken from suitable plants in spring and summer.

Which plants to use

This method suits the long stem growth of climbers such as clematis, ivy (*Hedera*) and honeysuckle (*Lonicera*). It also suits shrubs with hollow stems or those prone to rotting, such as camellia and mahonia.

Creating material for cuttings

No special preparation is required for just a few cuttings. If large numbers are required, prune shoots the previous summer to encourage more dormant buds into growth. Feed and water the plant well after pruning.

Selecting material

Select only stems that are healthy and growing true to type. Growth should be of the current season and can be softwood taken in spring, or semi-ripe growth taken in summer. Remove stems of climbers back to the old wood and make a number of cuttings along their length. Look for stems where the bud at the leaf apex is present.

Use sharp secateurs to remove stems from selected plants. When taking the material, always cut the stem just above a leaf node to leave the plant tidy with no short stem snags.

Preparing the cuttings

Trim the cuttings with a sharp knife by placing them on a clean, hard surface such as a wall tile. Cut just above a leaf or pair of leaves, taking care not to damage the leaf bud. Cut higher if the bud is large.

Make the lower cut on a node for hollow-stemmed plants, or between the nodes for climbers or where material is limited. The size of the cutting will depend on the distance between the nodes; 2.5 cm (1 in) of stem is probably the minimum size for successful rooting. Large leaves can be trimmed, or one of a pair removed, if the material is soft.

Dip the bases of the stems in rooting hormone and, if necessary, use a dibber to make a hole in the compost. Insert the cuttings so that the leaf bud is sitting just above the surface of the compost. The longer stems of clematis suit a deeper pot.

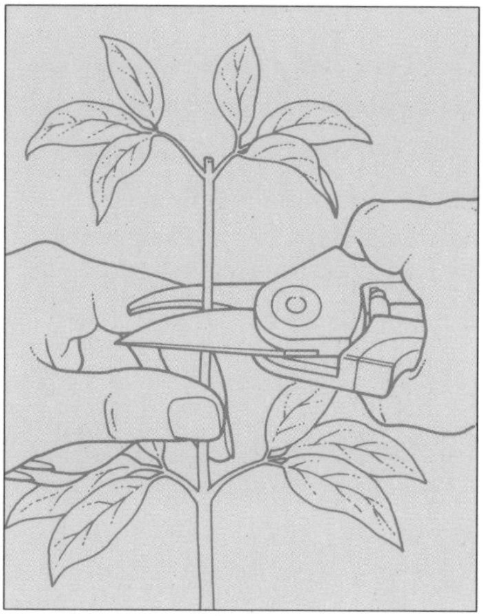

Taking internodal cuttings

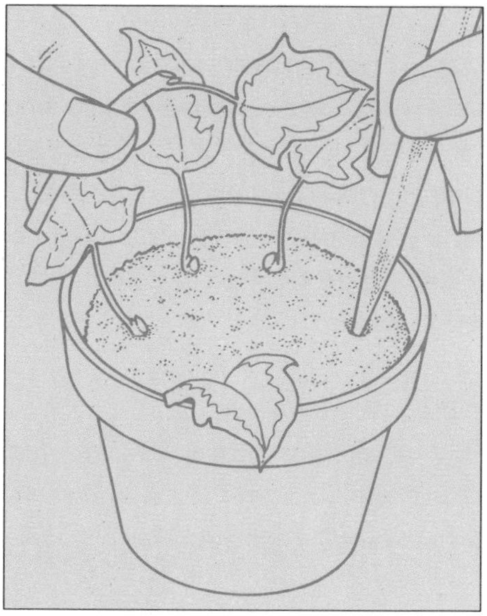

Insert cuttings up to the leaf bud

Continue to insert cuttings so that the leaves just avoid touching each other. Label, water the cuttings thoroughly using a fine spray from watering can or hose and then cover immediately.

Aftercare

As with softwood and semi-ripe cuttings, leaf bud cuttings can be encouraged to root in a range of different situations as long as the cuttings are covered to stay moist and kept warm at about 15°C (59°F).

Check for signs of rooting after about six weeks. When roots appear, pot the cuttings up individually and harden off before planting out the following season.

PLANTS SUITABLE FOR LEAF BUD CUTTINGS

Camellia	camellia
Clematis	clematis
Ficus elastica	rubber plant
Hedera	ivy
Lonicera	honeysuckle
Mahonia	Oregan grape
Parthenocissus	Virginia and Boston creeper
Vitis vinifera	grape vine

WHAT CAN GO WRONG

These cuttings can experience any of the problems found in softwood or semi-ripe cuttings.

HARDWOOD CUTTINGS

Hardwood cuttings are taken from woody plants when the stems are becoming firm and woody at the end of the first season of growth. New shoots that formed in spring have grown and matured through summer and by autumn have already become woody.

Cuttings are taken from autumn to spring when the plant is dormant. Rooting takes about six months. The woody outer layer on the stem, coupled with a slowing down of growth in the colder months, results in slow root development, but the cutting material itself is far better able to withstand moisture loss, so aftercare is less intense. Some plants, notably willow (*Salix*) and poplar (*Populus*), need very little care and will easily root from cut stems just pushed into the soil.

Which plants to use

Hardwood cuttings can be taken from evergreen or deciduous trees, shrubs and woody climbers using stems that have developed over the summer months. It is a good way to obtain a large number of young plants for hedging. Currants, gooseberries and some fruiting climbers are also propagated by this method, which can tie in with winter pruning.

If you are not sure where young wood meets old, trace down the shoot from the tip and look for a series of rings around the stem. There may be five or six very closely spaced together. These are the traces of the scales which covered the leaf bud at the tip of the stem the previous spring.

Creating material for cuttings

A hardwood cutting needs to be a least 15 cm (6 in) long, and often up to 30 cm (12 in) to be successful. This is because rooting is slower, so the cutting needs larger food reserves to sustain it over this period. Many plants will naturally produce some vigorous growth each year including roses, dogwoods (*Cornus*) and smoke bush (*Cotinus*). If the plant is slow-growing and young shoots are not reaching this length in a season, then the plant needs to be pruned to encourage more vigorous growth. Prune back one or two stems by a third to a half in spring, and follow with a balanced fertilizer and plenty of water. Vigorous shoots may appear from the cut stems, or from dormant buds on other stems encouraged to break after pruning.

Taking material for hardwood cuttings

Selecting material

Only select stems from plants that are healthy and growing true to type. Choose stems of about a pencil thickness and avoid thin, weak growth and any that has been shaded out as the stem may have insufficient food stores to sustain the cutting until roots and shoots develop.

Cut evergreen material in late autumn. Cuttings from deciduous plants are best taken just as the leaves fall in autumn or just prior to bud burst in late winter or early spring.

Use sharp secateurs to remove the stems from your selected plants. Always cut the stem just above a leaf node to leave the plant tidy with no stem snags. Where the current season's growth is vigorous, cut the whole stem and make several cuttings along its length.

Preparing the cuttings

Use secateurs to trim stems to just below a leaf node, making the cuttings 15–30 cm (6–12 in) long. Trim back any soft tips to a node. Remove the lower leaves of evergreens so that only about four remain.

If making several cuttings along a stem, make the top cut just above a node at a slant so that it sheds the rain. Take care to keep the bare stems of deciduous plants upright when making the cuttings. Dip cuttings in rooting hormone before planting.

Planting hardwood cuttings outdoors

Cuttings from many deciduous and evergreen plants will root in garden soil if it is well drained and in a sunny, open site.

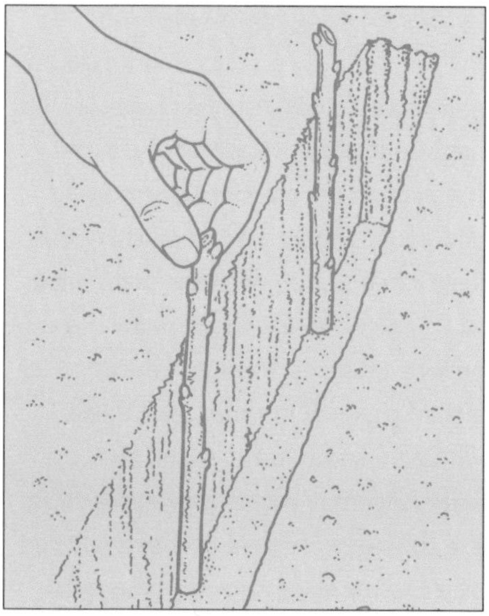

Inserting cuttings in a deep trench

Dig over the soil, adding organic matter or grit if necessary, then firm gently. Create a slit trench by driving a spade into the soil, then lever the spade backwards and forwards to open up a narrow slit. Move the spade sideways and repeat the action several times using a plank of wood as a guide to make a straight trench.

Put a layer of sharp sand in the base of the trench if extra drainage is required. Place the cuttings vertically in the trench so that two-thirds of their length is covered by soil. Space them 10 cm (4 in) apart. Replace the soil and firm it around the cuttings. Label and water thoroughly.

Planting hardwood cuttings in a cold frame

A cold frame set on a deep sand bed is perfect for rooting hardwood cuttings. Make a trench in the sand and insert the cuttings, following the instructions above for planting hardwood cuttings outdoors. The cold frame will offer protection from drying winds, freezing temperatures and heavy rains during the winter months which will benefit evergreen cuttings especially. In spring, new soft shoots can be shaded more easily and then later hardened off.

Alternatively, root the cuttings in deep pots placed in the cold frame. Select pots that are about 25 cm (10 in) deep, and part-fill with multi-purpose compost. Insert the prepared cuttings at about 5 cm (2 in) intervals, then top up with more compost. Water well and place in the cold frame.

Planting hardwood cuttings in a propagator

Some evergreens are difficult to root as hardwood cuttings and benefit from bottom heat. Insert prepared cuttings into deep pots of multipurpose compost and place them on a heated bench in a greenhouse, or in a heated propagator in a well-lit position. Water cuttings if they appear dry.

Planting hardwood cuttings in a sandbed

This is a useful technique if large numbers of cuttings are needed, perhaps for a hedge. Prepare the cuttings as usual, but tie them into bundles of about 15 stems. Bury the bundles in a box or raised bed of sand so that they don't dry out. By early spring, before the buds burst, check the lower cuts for signs of callusing. This will appear as a swollen, lumpy region due to rapid cell growth and from where roots are likely to emerge. Insert only those cuttings with a callus into slit trenches in a prepared outdoor bed for rooting.

PLANTS SUITABLE FOR HARDWOOD CUTTINGS

Actinidia	kiwi fruit
Buddleia	butterfly bush
Campsis	trumpet vine
Cornus alba, C. sericea	dogwood
Deutzia	deutzia
Ficus carica	fig tree
Garrya elliptica	silk tassel bush
Hydrangea	hydrangea
Ligustrum	privet
Lonicera	honeysuckle
Prunus	cherry, peach
Rosa	rose
Salix	willow
Santolina	cotton lavender
Viburnum	viburnum
Vitis	grape vine

WHAT CAN GO WRONG

LEAVES FALL OFF EVERGREEN OUTDOOR CUTTINGS

Problem: the cuttings have dried out
Action: try covering cuttings with a cloche, or place in a cold frame or greenhouse

BUDS FAIL TO OPEN TO PRODUCE NEW LEAVES, CUTTINGS FAIL TO ROOT

Problem: the soil is too wet or too dry
Action: improve soil drainage or cover cuttings to prevent drying out

Problem: cuttings are too small
Action: take cuttings of a good length from material that is about pencil thickness

Problem: cuttings have been inserted upside down
Action: check that stems are held upright when the cuttings are trimmed

BUDS OPEN, BUT SHRIVEL AND DIE

Problem: growth is fuelled by spring sunshine and food reserves in the cut stem, but root growth is still underdeveloped
Action: shade cuttings or consider rooting in a cooler position

Aftercare

Ensure that cuttings are kept moist; even deciduous stems can dry out in dry weather.

Don't be too eager to pot up the cuttings. New buds will burst into growth in spring, but often before the root system is well established. Shade new growth to prevent leaf scorch in the sun. Leave outdoor cuttings to grow through the summer until August when a good root system should have developed, then transplant to their final positions. Cuttings in a cold frame or pots can be potted up individually for planting out in the following spring.

Cuttings rooted in a propagator or greenhouse should be removed from the heat once they have developed a good root system and then maintained in a protected environment until spring. Pot up plants individually and grow on before planting out in autumn or the following spring.

Lilac plants can be propagated by root cuttings

ROOT CUTTINGS

Cuttings can be taken from the roots of certain plants during their dormant season, mostly in winter. Some plants will produce shoots from roots more readily than others. In many cases a plant's behaviour can be predicted by the way it grows in the garden. Some shrubs throw up shoots some distance from the main stem and if these are traced down to soil level, they are seen to emerge from underground roots. This can be seen as a nuisance, and is most notable in sumach (*Rhus typhina*) and lilac (*Syringa*). However, roots of this type of plant make ideal material for root cuttings and the method is very economical, producing plenty of new plants. The cuttings can often be taken without lifting an established plant, but roots should be less than a year old.

Which plants to use

This method is suitable for shrubs, trees and climbers that show a tendency to produce shoots (suckers) from the root system, but not those that sucker on the stem.

It is also successful with hardy perennials that form a rosette of top growth that is unsuitable for cuttings, and which dislike the root disturbance caused by division.

Preparing material for cuttings

No preparation is needed if only a few cuttings are required. On established trees or shrubs, one or two roots can be trimmed back in the spring to allow new roots to develop by winter.

Large amounts of new cutting material can be gained if hardy perennials are lifted the previous winter and the roots trimmed back to encourage plenty of new growth.

Selecting material

Select only stems from plants that are healthy and are growing true to type. Root cuttings from variegated plants will have plain leaves as the mutation causing variegation originates in the shoot tips and is not present in root growth. Select roots that are swollen as they will contain a store of food to fuel shoot growth. Discard any that are dark brown and woody.

Take the cuttings when the plant is dormant. This is usually between late autumn and early spring, but some spring-flowering plants may have a summer dormancy.

For established plants, carefully scrape away the soil from the root system to expose some paler fleshy roots. Clean away the soil and use sharp secateurs to cut the root straight across. Be sure that the cut roots are all aligned as they were on the plant, with the cut made closest to the main stem at the top.

Dig up hardy perennials to cause minimal root damage. If the soil is sticky, plunge the whole root system in a bucket of water to wash off some of the soil. Use sharp secateurs to remove lengths of fleshy roots as close to the crown of the plant as possible. Put the root lengths aside with the cut closest to the crown placed at the top.

Preparing the container

Fill seed trays or pots with a suitable compost. Plants that grow in well-drained soil will root more successfully in a well-drained compost. Try mixing sand, fine grit or perlite into multi-purpose compost to improve drainage.

Remove strong roots for trimming

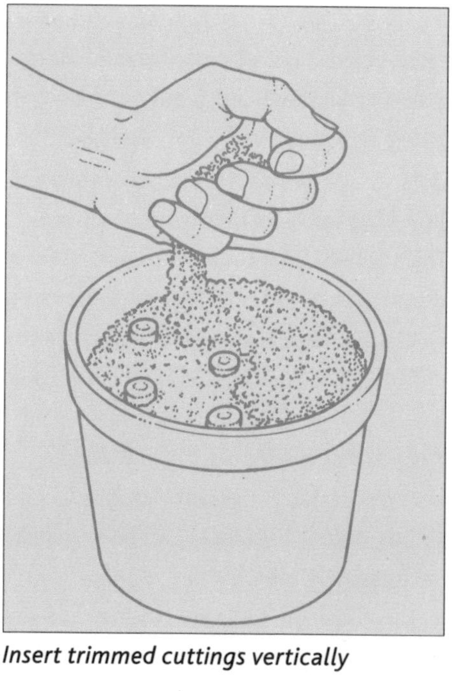

Insert trimmed cuttings vertically

Preparing the cuttings

Trim the cuttings by placing the roots onto a hard surface and use a sharp knife to remove fibrous side roots. Cut the roots to the required length by making the top cut straight across and the lower cut at a slant. This will remind you which way up the cuttings go.

The length of the root cuttings will depend on the thickness of the roots. Thicker roots can be cut into shorter lengths than thinner roots. The length is also related to the temperature of the rooting environment. If it is warm, the cutting can be just 2.5 cm (1 in) long and will new shoots develop quickly to fuel new root growth. If the temperature is low, the cutting won't produce shoots until spring so a larger food store in a larger root cutting of up to 10 cm (4 in) is needed.

Short root cuttings can be inserted into the compost vertically with the slanted cut below and the horizontal cut just level with the surface of the compost. Thin, fragile cuttings can be laid on the top of the compost.

Space the cuttings about 2.5 cm (1 in) apart and cover with a good layer of vermiculite to help retain moisture. Label and then water thoroughly.

Aftercare

Root cuttings can be placed in a variety of rooting environments that will affect the rate at which rooting occurs.

Either place on a heated bench in a greenhouse or in a heated propagator set at about 20°C (68°F) and keep just moist. Small shoots will start to appear first, followed by roots in as little as four weeks. Allow roots to develop well, then remove from the heat but keep protected until the spring. Pot up cuttings into individual pots when the shoots and new roots are large enough to handle. Harden off the plants before planting out when they are good size, which may be by late summer.

Alternatively, place cuttings in a cold frame and keep it closed during the winter months. Rooting will be slower at lower temperatures, but expect to see new shoots with a good root system by spring. When large enough to handle, the cuttings can be potted up individually and grown on before planting out.

WHAT CAN GO WRONG

CUTTINGS FAIL TO SHOOT

Problem: the compost is too wet, causing cuttings to rot

Action: water the compost so that it's just moist, or mix additives into the compost to provide extra drainage

Problem: the cuttings are too small for the temperature

Action: if you only have limited material available, place cuttings at a higher temperature or, if you can, make the cuttings bigger

PLANTS SUITABLE FOR ROOT CUTTINGS

Acanthus	bear's breeches
Anemone	anemone
Brunnera macrophylla	Siberian bugloss
Campsis	campsis
Dicentra	bleeding heart
Echinacea purpurea	purple coneflower
Echinops ritro	globe thistle
Eryngium	sea holly
Humulus lupulus	hop
Papaver orientale	oriental poppy
Phlox paniculata	border phlox
Primula denticulata	drumstick primula

You can also place cuttings of hardy plants in well-drained soil in a sheltered position outdoors, but expect greater losses. Cover the cuttings with a thin layer of soil, then with grit or fleece to provide extra protection against pest attack. Water only when necessary to keep the cuttings just moist. Shoots should appear after about three or four months, but don't be too quick to transplant as the new root system still has to develop fully.

Propagate Oriental poppies (Papaver orientale) by root cuttings

LEAF PETIOLE CUTTINGS

In a few cases, new plants can be encouraged to grow from just a leaf once it has been detached from the plant. Leaves are removed with a length of petiole, the stalk by which they are attached to the main plant. Amazingly, tiny new leaves grow from the cut petiole as the old leaf fades and dies away. Not surprisingly, this mechanism for survival is only seen in plants originating in warm, moist environments.

Which plants to use

Leaf petiole cuttings can be taken from a limited range of houseplants. African violet (*Saintpaulia*) is the most common example.

Preparing the container

Leaf petiole cuttings will be quite small, so you will be able to fit several in a 10 cm (4 in) pot. If you have more, use a standard or half seed tray for the cuttings. Fill the pot or tray with multi-purpose compost, adding up to a third perlite to improve drainage and prevent rotting.

Selecting material

Only select leaves that are healthy, true to type and fully expanded. Cuttings can be taken at any time of year, but spring or summer will provide good light levels to aid rooting.

Use a sharp knife to cut the leaf at the base of the petiole where it is attached to the main plant to keep the plant tidy. As the growth is soft, place cuttings in a plastic bag to prevent drying out if they are not to be inserted immediately.

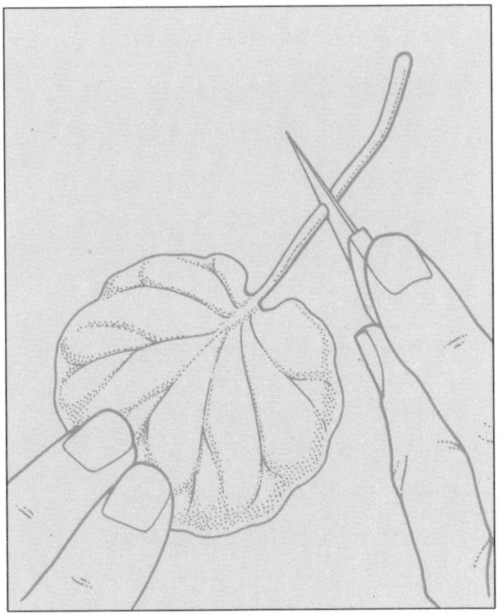

Trimming leaf petiole cuttings

Preparing the cuttings

Remove the leaf cuttings from the plastic bag a few at a time. Place them on a hard surface such as a wall tile and trim the petioles about 2.5 cm (1 in) below the leaf. Leave the petioles longer on larger leaves to help support them in the compost.

Use a dibber to make a hole in the compost and place the petiole into the hole so that leaf sits at a slight angle from vertical. The lower edge of the leaf should be just above the compost surface. Gently firm the compost around the petiole using the dibber. Repeat with further cuttings, spacing them about 2.5 cm (1 in) apart. Water the compost but try to avoid wetting the leaves if they have a hairy surface as they will rot easily. Cover with a plastic bag or rigid plastic pot cover.

Aftercare

As the parent plants require warm conditions, so the cuttings must also be kept at about 20°C (68°F) for rooting to occur. Keep them slightly moist in a well-lit position, perhaps a warm, bright windowsill. Pots or trays could also be placed in a propagator in a greenhouse or conservatory. A heated propagator will be necessary in the cooler months but not in summer.

Only water the cuttings if they start to look dry. Look out for the first signs of shoot growth at compost level after two or three months, but leave them undisturbed as they grow slowly. Don't worry about the appearance of the original leaf; it will continue to deteriorate and can be removed when it eventually dies.

Cuttings can be potted up individually after about four months, once they are large enough to handle. Cuttings placed individually in pots can remain there for longer but water in a weak houseplant feed during the growing season.

Insert cuttings near vertically

WHAT CAN GO WRONG

CUTTINGS BEGIN TO ROT

Problem: the compost is too wet, allowing fungal rots to take hold

Action: water only to keep the compost just moist, or mix extra drainage materials into the compost

CUTTINGS FAIL TO ROOT

Problem: cuttings failed to root before the leaf dried out

Action: check the environment is warm enough for the selected plant

LEAF BLADE CUTTINGS

This involves cutting the leaf blade into sections and bringing these into contact with the compost to allow new shoots and roots to develop at the cut edges of the veins. The leaf can be cut in a number of ways, but the exposed veins need to be in contact with the compost in warm and humid conditions for the technique to be successful. As with leaf petiole cuttings, only plants from warm, moist climates have the ability to propagate in this way.

Which plants to use

Some commonly grown houseplants can be propagated by this method. Begonias and streptocarpus are the most popular varieties.

Preparing the container

Depth of container is not important as the leaves are laid on the surface of the compost. Use 10 cm (4 in) pots if you have just a few cuttings, potting them up individually, or seed trays if you have quite a few. Use multi-purpose compost, adding up to a third perlite to improve drainage. Fill the pots or trays with the compost and tamp down.

Selecting material

Leaf blade cuttings can be taken at any time of year, but spring or summer will provide good light levels to promote rooting.

Select only healthy leaves which are true to type and fully expanded. Use a sharp knife to cut the leaf at the base of the leaf stalk (petiole) where it is attached to the main plant to keep the plant tidy. As the growth is soft, place cuttings in a plastic bag to prevent drying out if they are not to be inserted immediately.

Preparing the cuttings

There are several methods which can be used to cut the leaf and make a good number of cuttings from which to generate new plants.

Leaf slashing

This is a very effective technique when used with begonias, especially *Begonia rex*. Lay the leaf upside down on a large tile to expose the underside. Use a sharp knife to make a series of cuts into the larger, more prominent leaf veins, spacing the cuts about 2.5 cm (1 in) apart. Try not to cut through the leaf completely so that it is not too heavily damaged.

Trim back the leaf stalk (petiole) to where it joins the leaf blade. Water the compost so that it is just moist, turn over the leaf and place it face up on the compost surface.

Ensure the cut veins are in contact with the compost by weighting the leaf down with one or two small stones, or using pieces of bent wire pressed into the compost to hold it in place.

Leaf squares

This method is also effective for begonias. Lay the leaf upside down on a tile to expose the underside. Using a ruler as a guide, cut the leaf into 2.5 cm (1 in) strips with a main vein down the middle of each. Cut across the strips to create squares of leaf. Leave the squares in position for the time being, as you will need to know which way round they go.

Use the ruler to make shallow furrows in the compost, and place a leaf square vertically in the furrow so that the cut edge that was originally closest to the leaf base is at the bottom of the furrow. Leave about three-quarters of the leaf square exposed, and firm it in gently. Repeat with the other squares, spacing them roughly 2.5 cm (1 in) apart, then water well.

Leaf slices

This method is similar to the leaf squares method, but is used on plants with narrow leaves. Lay the leaf upside down on a large tile to expose the underside. Using a ruler as a straight edge, cut across the leaf to create 2.5 cm (1 in) deep slices.

Use the ruler to make shallow furrows in the compost, and place a leaf slice vertically into the furrow so that the cut edge closest to the base of the leaf is in the compost.

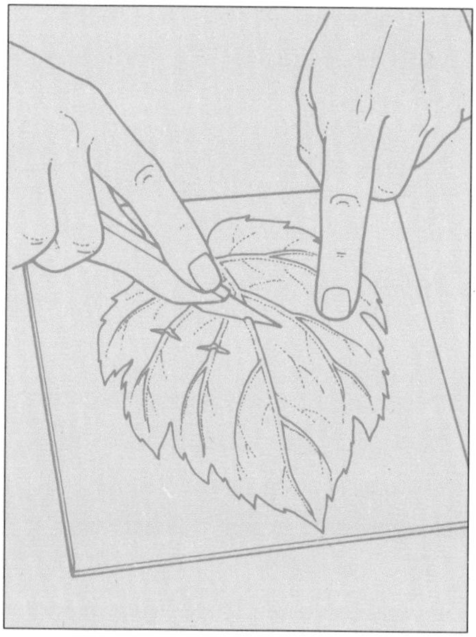

Cutting through the leaf veins

Inserting the squares vertically

Leave about three-quarters of the leaf slice exposed and firm it in gently. Repeat with the other slices, spacing them roughly 2.5 cm (1 in) apart, then water well.

Aftercare

Treat leaf blade cuttings in the same way as leaf petiole cuttings (see page 69).

PLANTS SUITABLE FOR LEAF BLADE CUTTINGS

Begonia rex	rex begonia
Begonia masoniana	iron cross begonia
Hoya	wax flower
Kalanchoe	kalanchoe
Sanseveria	mother-in-law's tongue
Schlumbergia	Christmas cactus
Streptocarpus x hybridus	streptocarpus

WHAT CAN GO WRONG

LEAF SECTIONS ROT

Problem: the compost is too wet or the conditions too humid, allowing fungal diseases to take hold
Action: water only to keep the compost just moist, or improve drainage

Problem: leaf sections are buried too deeply
Action: be sure to only bury a small amount of the leaf surface

CUTTINGS FAIL TO ROOT

Problem: the temperature for rooting is too low
Action: move to a heated propagator or wait until the summer months

Problem: cuttings have been placed in the compost upside down
Action: be sure to keep cuttings arranged to that the base is easily identified

CUTTINGS DIE AFTER POTTING UP INDIVIDUALLY

Problem: rooted cuttings were too small to be disturbed
Action: be sure that individual plants have developed a good root system before potting

DIVISION

Division is an easy way to create new plants from those already growing in the garden. It can be carried out successfully without any special equipment and is met with success almost every time.

Division is a fairly straightforward process of splitting a plant into pieces. Each section has a root and a shoot or shoot bud, so that it can survive as an independent plant. As the new plants already have a root system in place, this is a reliable method and generally successful even for beginners. Also, the new plants will reach a good size more quickly than those grown from seed or cuttings, so it yields quicker returns.

What to divide

Division works with plants that display a specific growth habit. They are perennials that produce a wealth of growth buds at the crown, which develop into stems or rosettes of leaves at or close to soil level. It is a very easy and popular method of propagating herbaceous perennials and grasses but the technique can also be used for shrubs with a suckering growth habit. The main requirements are that the plant is big enough to be divided and that the divisions are big enough to grow on independently.

PLANTS IN THE BORDER

As border perennials grow and increase in size, they lend themselves to division. For some plants this is a necessary part of their maintenance. Many can show reduced flowering as they become congested, and others die off in the centre as they grow outwards. Whether division is for maintenance or for propagation, dig the whole plant out of the soil to divide it and only select healthy sections from the plant, discarding material from the dead central region. Replant these healthy sections back into the border as required.

PLANTS IN POTS

Large plants bought at a nursery or garden centre may be big enough to divide before they are planted out. Look for healthy plants with several shoots and a good root system. The divisions can either be planted out straight away or they can be grown on in pots until they are big enough to plant out.

Sweet Laura (Alstroemeriea) in a border

Cranesbill (Geranium) is suitable for division

When to divide

The best time to divide established plants in the border is in the spring or autumn. This avoids the extreme cold and possible frozen ground of winter and the heat and dryness of summer.

In spring the majority of plants support fewer leaves and their absence will help reduce the moisture loss from the plant when its water uptake is reduced due to minor disturbance and damage of its roots.

In early autumn, plants are in the process of dying back and losing leaves so water loss will be reduced then too. The soil will still be warm enough for roots to grow into the surrounding soil.

A few plants are better divided in the summer as at this time the divisions will establish more readily.

Size of divisions

The size of the final divisions will depend on the final position of the plant and its vigour. If you intend to replant the divisions into a fertile, well-drained soil in spring or autumn, divisions will grow well if kept watered. In this case, the divisions can be quite small.

If you are replanting the divisions into a poorly drained soil in autumn as the soil is cooling, a bigger division with a bigger root system may have a better chance of survival than smaller sections.

To achieve larger numbers of new plants from one parent plant, make smaller divisions and grow them on in individual pots of compost. Place them in a warm position to promote the growth of new roots and shoots: a greenhouse or cold frame in spring or autumn will help. The new plants will be ready to plant out when the roots fill a 9 cm (3½ in) pot, but they can be grown on into larger pots if preferred.

HARDY PERENNIALS WITH FIBROUS ROOTS

A typical hardy perennial ripe for division will produce a cluster of shoots or leaf rosettes above ground, supported by a tangle of fairly fine roots below.

Prepare the plant

Before lifting the plant from the border, the root system needs to be exposed. Dig the soil around the established plant with a spade or border fork to gently loosen it and release some of the finer roots. Use a border fork to lever the rootball out of the soil. Direct the tines at the base of the plant and insert to their full length. Use the handle to lever the fork up and down to gently loosen the bigger roots.

Work around the plant, following the same procedure until the rootball is released and is ready for lifting. The ease by which the plant is released from the soil depends on how long the plant has been left growing unhindered, the size of the rootball, the strength of the root system and the stickiness of the soil.

Divide the plant

For small root systems, rosettes or leafy stems can be teased apart by hand or with the help of a hand fork. Work gently to allow the shoots and roots to untangle rather than break. Be wary of separating out the pieces so vigorously that shoots or roots break off as these will need to be discarded.

For large root systems, more effort may be needed to break open the tangle of roots. If you can get hold of them, place two garden forks back to back into the centre of the rootball. Gently lever the handles apart from each other and then pull them together. As

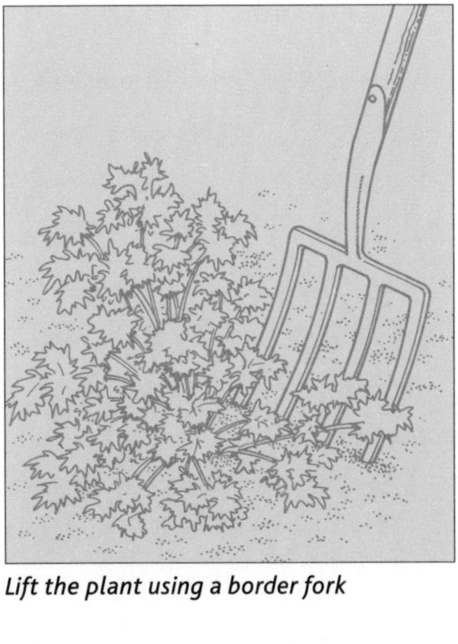

Lift the plant using a border fork

Small plants may be separated by hand

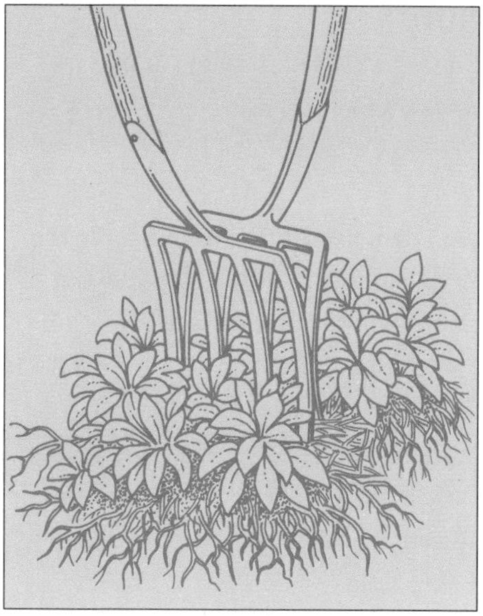

Use two forks to tease apart tough roots

the rootball starts to loosen, try pulling the handles together and then move on past each other. The curve on the fork tines will push the rootball apart and into two pieces without any strain on the back.

The same technique can be used again to split the divisions further until the roots and shoots can be teased apart by hand.

Aftercare

If the sections are being returned to the border, dig over the soil, incorporating some well-rotted organic matter, then replant at the same depth as before. Water well and keep watered in the first few weeks if the weather is dry.

If sections are to be potted up, use a multipurpose compost and water the plants well. Keep watered if under cover and move outside when they have put out new growth. Place pots in a sheltered spot to grow on. A greenhouse or coldframe would be ideal but lined up at the base of a house wall will do. Keep them well ventilated and plant out when they have put out some growth.

WHAT CAN GO WRONG

DIVISION FAILS TO GROW

Problem: the root system struggles to survive adverse conditions
Action: avoid dividing in autumn if the soil becomes cold and wet soon after planting. Remember to water divisions made in spring during dry periods

Problem: the root system on the division is too small to be replanted in open ground
Action: pot up divisions and grow on for a season until the roots have become better established

HARDY PERENNIALS WITH FIBROUS ROOTS

Alchemilla mollis	lady's mantle
Aster	michaelmas daisy
Campanula	bell flower
Geranium	cranesbill
Geum	avens
Leucanthemum	shasta daisy
Rudbeckia	coneflower
Sedum spectabile	ice plant
Stachys byzantina	lamb's ears

HARDY PERENNIALS WITH FLESHY ROOTS

Only when the root system of a perennial is exposed will it be apparent if the main roots are large and fleshy with only a few fibrous roots present. Look out for growth buds to decide how many divisions can be made from the parent plant.

Prepare the plant

Lift the plant from the border, following the same method as for fibrous-rooted perennials (see page 77). Take extra care as plants with fleshy roots can be more difficult to extract and some roots might break off.

Divide the plant

Rather than being teased apart, the fleshy roots need to be cut into sections with a sharp blade so that each section of root supports at least one growth bud, preferably more. It may be necessary to shake or wash off some of the soil to expose the roots and allow for a cleaner cut.

For small root systems, use a sharp garden knife to cut vertically down the root from the crown to create the divisions.

For larger root systems, place the rootball upright on a firm surface and cut down sharply with a garden spade. Make sure that the blade is sharp so that a clean cut is made, rather than bruising which may cause dieback of some roots. Make further cuts as necessary to create small divisions as required.

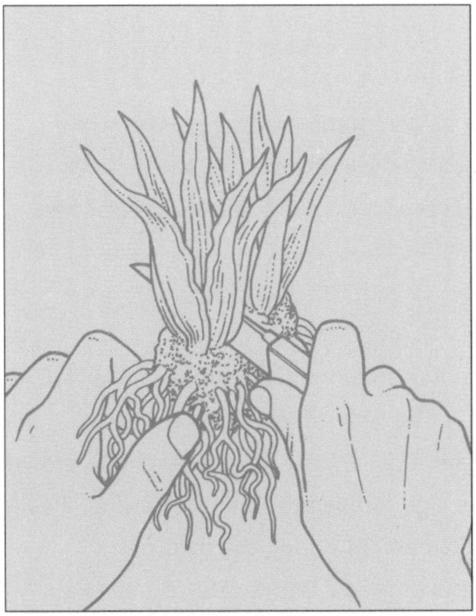

Use a sharp knife to cut through fleshy roots

For tougher root systems, you will need to use a spade

Aftercare

Large divisions can be replanted into the border. Dig over the soil and incorporate some well-rotted manure before replanting. The hole should be large enough and deep enough to accommodate roots that may appear slightly cumbersome. Gently firm the soil around the roots and water well for several weeks if the weather is dry.

WHAT CAN GO WRONG

DIVISION FAILS TO GROW

Problem: the root system struggles to survive adverse conditions
Action: avoid dividing in autumn if the soil becomes cold and wet soon after planting. Remember to water divisions made in spring during dry periods

Problem: the root system is too small for the division to be replanted in open ground
Action: pot up divisions and grow on for a season until the roots have become better established

HARDY PERENNIALS WITH FLESHY ROOTS

Aconitum	monkshood
Aruncus	goatsbeard
Astilbe	astilbe
Canna	canna
Helleborus	hellebore
Hemerocallis	daylily
Hosta	plantain lily
Kniphofia	red hot poker
Liatris	blazing star
Zantedeschia	arum lily

GRASSES

Of the ornamental grass-like plants used in the garden, some are true grasses while others are simply perennials with narrow strap-shaped leaves. Many of these plants can be divided by cutting or teasing apart, but others produce a solid tangle of fine white fibrous roots that pose more of a problem.

Prepare the plant

Lift the plant from the border or remove it from its container in the same way as for hardy perennials with fibrous roots (see page 77). The time of year can be very important to the survival of divisions from grasses. Cool season grasses start into growth in early spring, and are past their best when the high temperatures arrive, having already flowered. These can be divided at any time of year, except during the heat of midsummer. However, many grasses that we grow originate from hotter climates and don't start into growth until the beginning of summer, flowering towards the end or into autumn. These need to be divided as they start into growth in early summer.

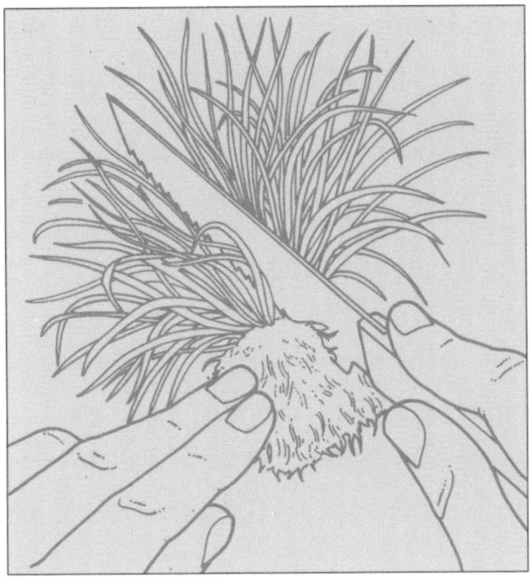

Saw through the root mat

Divide the plant

For small plants or where the roots are fine and fibrous, saw the rootball into pieces using an old bread knife. The divisions can be cut to produce small plants down to 2.5 cm (1 in) in diameter if required, although at this size plants should be potted up and grown on to ensure success.

Larger grasses can be cut with a sharp-bladed spade or knife to produce sections no smaller than 5 cm (2 in) in diameter as smaller pieces often die off.

GRASSES WITH A FINE ROOT MAT

Cool season grasses to divide in spring:

Briza	quaking grass
Calamagrostis x acutiflora	reed grass
Festuca	fescue
Hakonechloa	hakonechloa
Milium effusum 'Aureum'	golden wood millet
Phalaris arundinacea	gardener's garters
Stipa	feather grass

Hot season grasses to divide in summer:

Cortaderia	pampas grass
Elymus	lyme grass
Imperata	imperata
Miscanthus	miscanthus
Pennisetum	fountain grass

Hakonechloa macra 'Aureola'

WHAT CAN GO WRONG

DIVISIONS FAIL TO GROW

Problem: the divisions have been made too small or made at the wrong time of year

Action: observe the growth habit of the grass and divide when it is in growth, but don't be too greedy

Very large and well established grasses such as pampas grass (*Cortaderia*) are virtually impossible to lift from the soil without resorting to a pick axe. Divisions may become available during the demolition process.

SUCKERING SHRUBS

Some shrubs throw up several stems directly from the ground rather than branch from a single stem. These are known as suckering shrubs and are often the same shrubs that show a 'running' tendency, as the roots extend away from the main plant and then throw up new shoots. A section of roots and shoots can be cut away from the main plant with a sharp-bladed spade and be transplanted elsewhere or potted up to make a new plant.

Remove the sucker by cutting the root

Prepare the plant

There is no need to lift the shrub from the ground, but you will have to remove soil to expose the root when the cut is to be made.

Divide the plant

Use a sharp-bladed spade to chop through the exposed root section. It will probably take several attempts to cut right through. Dig up the severed section, taking care not to damage the roots too much.

WHAT CAN GO WRONG

DIVIDED SUCKER DIES

Problem: the root system is too small to support the existing top growth

Action: cut back top growth and consider potting up small divisions to grow on before planting out

SUCKERING SHRUBS

Amelanchier	snowy mespilus
Aronia	chokeberry
Cornus stolonifera	dogwood
Hypericum calycinum	rose of Sharon
Kerria japonica	jew's mantle
Rosa rugosa	hedgehog rose
Symphoricarpus	snowberry

Aftercare

The section can be replanted in a new position in the garden. Dig over the soil well and incorporate some organic matter, such as well-rotted manure. Plant the section to the same depth as it was before. As the root system may be quite shallow, reduce the height of tall stems to about 30 cm (12 in) to reduce the likelihood of root rock until the plant has become established.

Smaller sections can be potted up and grown on, but cut back tall stems to just above the compost level to reduce water loss as the roots establish themselves.

PLANTS WITH FLESHY RHIZOMES

A rhizome is a swollen stem in which food is stored by the plant. The structure may sit underground or just on the soil surface, but is usually horizontal with shoots rising vertically from it. A rhizome houses dormant buds along its length just like a normal stem, so if it is cut into sections, it can be used to create a number of new plants.

Prepare the plant

Lift the plant from the soil or remove it from its container carefully so as not to break the rhizome. A well-established plant in the border may be growing from a congested tangle of rhizomes, which will take some time to release from the soil.

Divide the plant

Use a sharp-bladed knife to cut the rhizome into sections, ensuring that the cuts are clean. Examine the rhizomes and make sure each section has at least two growth buds,

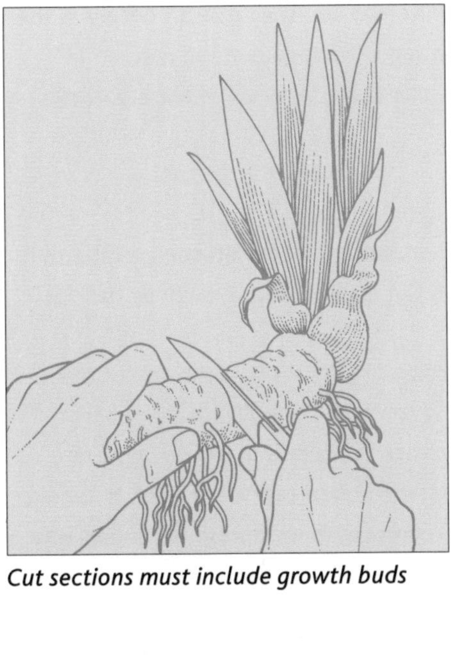

Cut sections must include growth buds

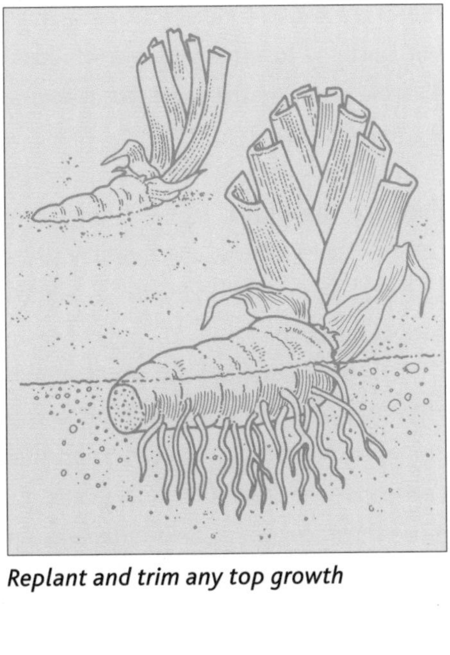

Replant and trim any top growth

as well as plenty of roots growing from it.

Smaller sections are less likely to survive as they will have a limited food store, and a section with no apparent growth bud won't be able to produce shoots.

Aftercare

If the plant is in leaf, cut back the top growth by half to reduce the stress of water loss while the roots are still recovering. Replant new sections in the border into a patch of well dug soil into which you have incorporated plenty of organic matter such as well-rotted manure. Plant the rhizome sections at the same level as before division. Water well and regularly until the plants are established.

WHAT CAN GO WRONG

RHIZOME SECTION DOESN'T GROW

Problem: the cut section doesn't contain a dormant bud

Action: cut the rhizomes into large sections, so even if you can't see a bud or two there will probably be some present

PLANTS WITH FLESHY RHIZOMES

Aspidistra	cast iron plant
Bergenia	elephant's ears
Iris, bearded types	iris
Polygonatum	solomon's seal
Polypodium	polypody fern
Trillium	wake robin

PLANTS WITH TUBERS

Tubers are swollen underground structures like rhizomes, but they may sit deeper in the soil, clustered together with growth buds also sitting close together. The method of division is broadly the same, but many tuberous plants are tender so plant preparation is slightly different.

Prepare the plant

Lift the plant from the soil carefully to reduce root damage. Shake off some of the soil to expose the tubers and make separation easier. Cut back the top growth by half for ease of handling.

If the plant is tender and needs winter protection, lift the plant at the end of the growing season as normal. Trim off any remaining top growth and leave the tubers to dry off so that the dry soil can be brushed away. Pack the tubers in dry compost or newspaper and store as normal in a cool, dry frost-free place over the winter. In spring, move them to a warm, well-lit position in moist compost to encourage the tubers into growth.

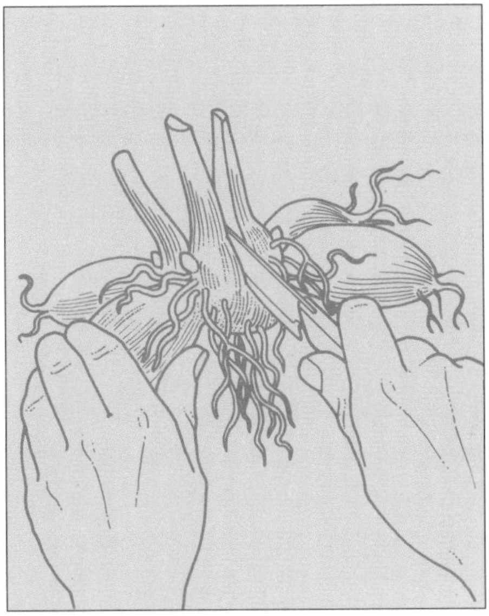

__Dahlia:__ cut between tubers

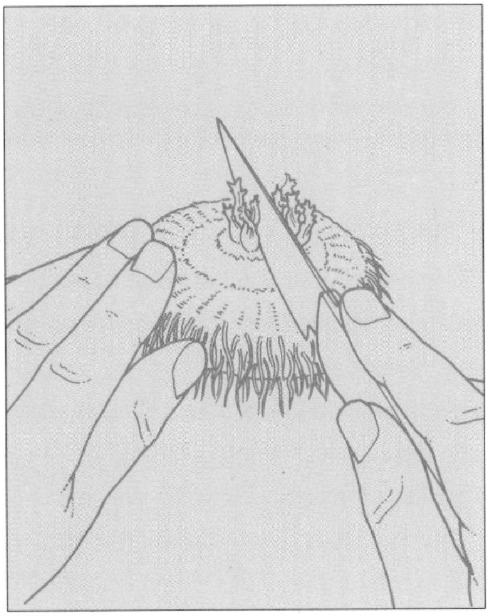

__Begonia:__ cut the tuber in half

Divide the plant

For dahlias, use a sharp knife to cut the tubers into sections, each of which must have a growing shoot. If no shoot is apparent on a tuber, leave it attached to one that does have a growing shoot. This is often the case on the smaller, less developed tubers. Repot the divided tubers into pots of compost.

For plants such as begonia where the tuber increases every year, cut the tuber in half, taking care that each half supports one or more growing shoots. If possible, treat the cut surface with fungicide and repot the divisions into compost.

WHAT CAN GO WRONG

TUBER ROTS IN STORAGE

Problem: the compost is too wet or the atmosphere too damp

Action: let the tuber dry out before storage, then check every few weeks

TUBER ROTS IN THE GROUND

Problem: the tuber is vulnerable to fungal disease in poorly drained soil

Action: plant when the soil is warm, and add extra drainage material

Aftercare

Replant hardy tuberous plant divisions into well-prepared soil in the border. Once the danger of frost has passed,

SUITABLE PLANTS

Begonia	tuberous begonia
Crocosmia	montbretia
Dahlia	dahlia
Gladiolus	gladioli

tender tubers can be hardened off and planted outside into well-prepared soil. Take care not to damage the young shoots. Small divisions made early in spring can be grown on in pots in multipurpose compost to allow the plants to mature enough to withstand outdoor conditions.

PLANTS WITH OFFSETS OR RUNNERS

The growth habit of plants that produce offsets is similar in appearance to that of suckering shrubs. The plant produces a main clump of shoots in the centre, but a few may appear away from the main group (known as offsets) as the plant spreads to cover more ground. It is a term used most often in relation to houseplants, succulents and low-growing rock plants and alpines. The structure on which the shoot or leaf rosette is attached is usually below the ground.

Plants that produce runners put out horizontal stems which produce roots and new shoots where the nodes touch the soil.

Prepare the plant

The plant can remain in the border or in its container. Once offsets or runners form, encourage them to root by bringing them into contact with soil or compost either by raising the level of compost or firming them into the soil.

If the offset is attached below soil level, scrape away the soil or compost to expose the sucker and check that there are roots attached. Check that the offsets or runners sitting above soil level are anchored by roots.

Rooted runners are easily detached

WHAT CAN GO WRONG

OFFSETS DIE AFTER PLANTING

Problem: the offsets have dried out as the root system is too small, or the soil has been allowed to dry out

Action: keep the new offsets watered until the root system is well established

Strawberries are renewed by runners

PLANTS WITH OFFSETS OR RUNNERS

Agave	agave
Ajuga reptans	bugle
Aloe	aloe
Chlorophytum	spider plant
Clivia	clivia
Fragaria	strawberry
Musa	banana
Saxifraga stolonifera	saxifrage
Sempervivum	houseleek

Divide the plant

Cut away the offset or runner with a sharp knife so that it has a good supply of roots attached. Gently ease the soil or compost from around the roots so that the offset can be removed without damage.

Aftercare

Plant the single offsets into well-prepared soil or compost that suits the plant. Houseplants can be potted up and grown on; succulents and alpines can be grown in compost with extra grit added.

BULBS THAT FORM CLUMPS

As bulbs and corms reach maturity, they increase in size and then start to produce small bulbs or corms which remain attached to the parent. These extra smaller growths will grow into the surrounding soil and eventually form a large congested clump which may fail to flower well. These newer bulbs or corms can be removed to a fresh site to grow on into mature flowering plants.

Prepare the plant

Most bulbs are best divided just as they die back and become dormant. The timing will vary with individual bulbs, depending on when they flower.

Carefully fork around the edge of the clump to loosen the soil. Dig under the clump using the fork as a lever to loosen the deep roots. Be careful not to damage new bulbs and corms that form below the older parents. Lift the clump free and remove loose soil.

Divide the plant

Separate the young bulbs and corms by hand from the parents. If they prove to be very strongly attached, use a knife to cut them away.

Aftercare

The larger bulbs and corms will probably be near flowering size and can be replanted in borders along with the parents. Dig over the soil and incorporate some well-rotted organic matter before planting. Smaller offsets can be grown on in pots for a year or two, then planted out once they have reached a good size.

Divide clumps of bulbs after flowering

Daffodils have bulbs that form clumps

BULBS THAT FORM CLUMPS

Camassia	quamash
Chionodoxa	glory of the snow
Colchicum	autumn crocus
Erythronium	dog's tooth violet
Galanthus	snowdrop
Muscari	grape hyacinth
Narcissus	daffodil
Scilla	squill

WHAT CAN GO WRONG

BULBS FAIL TO FLOWER

Problem: the smaller bulbs are too immature to flower

Action: continue to care for the smaller bulbs and they will bulk up to flowering size after a few more years

LAYERING

The general principle of layering is to encourage new roots to form on a stem while it is still attached to the parent plant. The stem normally grows above soil level and won't usually develop roots in this position, but root development is promoted when it is brought into contact with a rooting medium (soil or compost). The stem can then be severed and is immediately able to support itself on its own root system, unlike cuttings where the stem is severed without a root system in place. This might seem to describe the runners seen on strawberry plants, but these produce both shoots and roots at the same point on the stem and are classed as offsets (see page 86) which are propagated by division. Layering is usually carried out on established woody outdoor plants including trees, shrubs and climbers but it can also be used on certain woody-stemmed houseplants.

Layering is, in theory, an easy way to gain new plants as the stem continues to receive water and nutrients from the parent plant while a new root system forms. In reality, however, rooting is often slow and the amount of suitable material per plant may be small. You may come across a plant that has layered itself without any intervention, and this is natural in many plants when low-growing stems come in contact with the soil.

Various techniques can be employed to increase the chances of success with layering. Rooting is always more successful when stems are less than one year old, so the plant can be pruned and then the new shoots that grow as a result can be used for layering. Another trick is to remove a section of bark or cut into the stem where it comes into contact with the rooting medium to expose the core and encourage roots to form.

There are also methods to place the stem in contact with the rooting medium. The stem can be lowered to below soil level or bent several times to sit in and out of the soil several times along its length. Conversely, the rooting medium can be taken to meet the stem. For some plants, the soil is brought into contact with all the stems on the plant either by raising soil levels or lowering the whole plant into the ground.

SIMPLE LAYERING

This is the most straightforward method of layering and involves taking a young, pliable stem and bending it to bury part in the soil and leave the tip exposed.

This method is carried out in spring and is most suited to trees and shrubs where shoots emerge less than 30 cm (12 in) above soil level. The shoot needs to be 60–90 cm (2–3 ft) long and less than two years old. It must be pliable enough to be buried in the ground and then bent at right angles so that the shoot tip is facing upwards. If no such

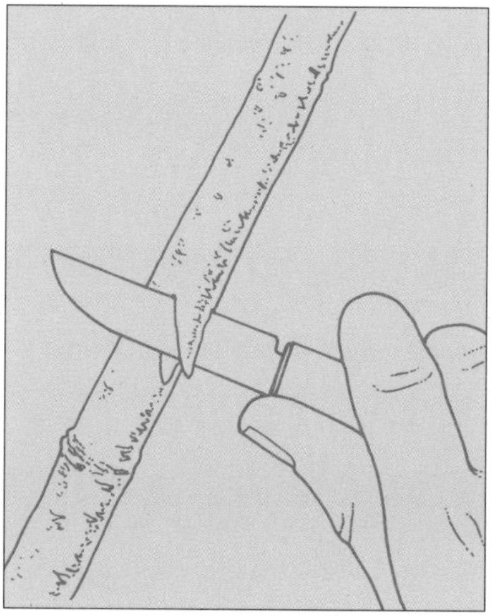

Wound the stem to aid rooting

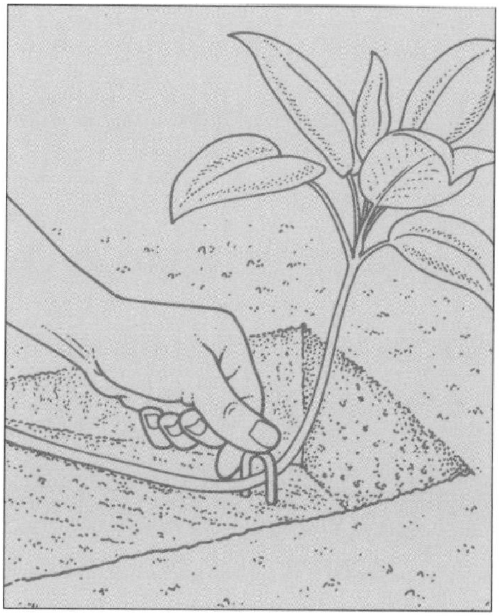

Secure the young stem in the soil and cover

PLANTS SUITABLE FOR SIMPLE LAYERING	
Actinidia	kiwi fruit
Amelanchier	snowy mespilus
Aucuba	spotted laurel
Corylopsis	corylopsis
Cotinus	smoke bush
Daphne	daphne
Erica	heather
Forsythia	forsythia
Lonicera	honeysuckle
Magnolia	magnolia
Rhododendron	rhododendron
Ribes	currants, gooseberry
Stephanandra	stephanandra
Syringa	lilac
Vaccinium	blueberry
Viburnum	viburnum
Vitis	grape vine

shoots are available, prune the plant hard in spring by cutting back side shoots close to the main branch. The vigorous new shoots that appear can be layered the following spring.

Method

In spring, inspect the plant for a likely shoot. Flex the stem to see where it will touch the soil. Dig over the soil in this area to a depth of 30 cm (12 in) and incorporate some multi-purpose compost and grit for extra drainage if the soil is sticky and wet. Make a 7.5 cm (3 in) deep trench in the soil and locate which part of the stem will sit below the soil.

Remove any leaves from the part of the stem to be buried. Wound the stem where it will sit horizontally below soil level to aid root development at this point by using a sharp knife to trim away some of the thin bark layer on the lower side. Alternatively, make a diagonal cut at the node half way through the stem. Apply rooting hormone to the cut surfaces.

Secure the stem in the soil using bent wire formed into pins or a suitably heavy stone, then back-fill with soil forming a slight mound to allow for settlement. Insert a cane close to the buried stem and tie the end of the stem to the cane so that the shoot is almost upright. Be careful not to dislodge the buried section. This will form the main stem of the new plant.

Aftercare

Water the area well and keep it moist, especially through the summer. Check the soil mound continues to cover the buried stem and keep the area free from weeds.

Look for new growth at the tip of the buried shoot, a sign that rooting has been successful. It may take as long as 12 months to form a sufficiently large root system, after which time you can sever the stem between parent and new plant.

Leave the new plant undisturbed for a few months more before transplanting or potting up to grow on.

SERPENTINE LAYERING

This method builds on simple layering as it involves bending and burying the stem several times along its length, so producing a greater number of new plants. As the stem needs to be long and flexible for this technique, it is used mainly for climbing plants.

Creating material for layering

Serpentine layering requires a shoot close to the ground which was made the previous year. If all new growth is high on the plant, prune selected stems hard to the ground to encourage new shoots from the base for layering the following year.

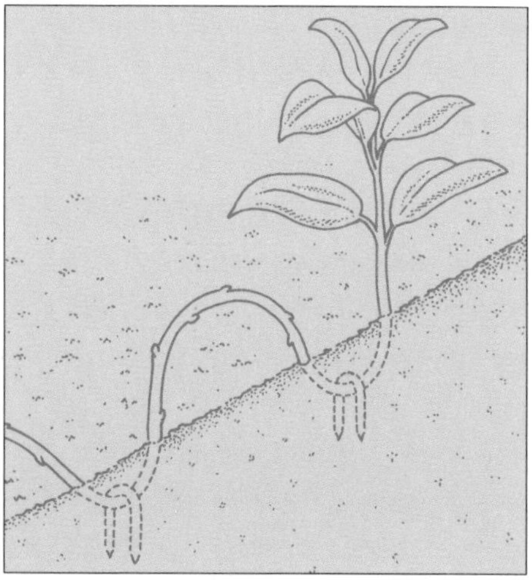

Secure the stem between leaf joints

Method

In spring, select a shoot of growth made in the previous year. Dig over the soil where the serpentine layer can run to a depth of 30 cm (12 in) and incorporate some multi-purpose compost and grit for extra drainage if the soil is sticky and wet.

Starting at the base of the shoot, wound the stem between leaf nodes by removing a sliver of bark or by cutting into the stem with a sharp knife. Apply rooting hormone to each cut.

Bend the stem to bury the wounded sections, but leave the unwounded sections, where leaves are attached, exposed above soil level. Pin the shoot in place using pieces of bent wire over the wounded sections. Gently cover with soil, leaving the stem tip above soil level.

Aftercare

Keep well watered, especially through the summer. Check the soil continues to cover the buried sections of stem and keep the area weed free.

Look for signs of new growth at the leaf joints and the tip of the buried shoot, a sign that rooting has been successful. Rooting may take place by autumn or not until the following spring.

Wait for a sufficiently large root system to form before severing the stem between parent and each adjacent new plant, just above a leaf joint. Pot up new plants to grow on for another season before planting out.

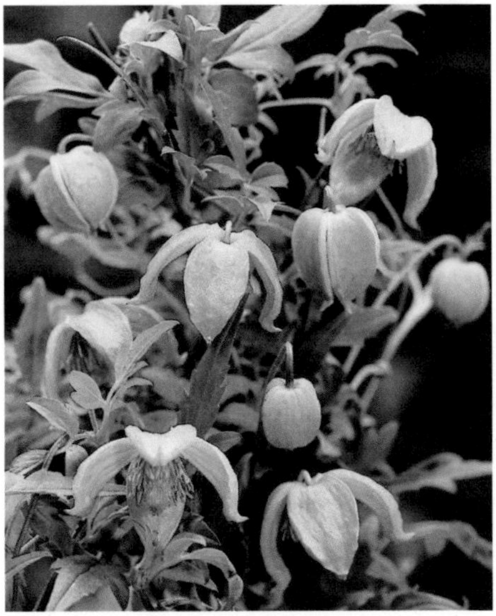

Propagate Clematis by layering

PLANTS SUITABLE FOR SERPENTINE LAYERING

Clematis	clematis
Humulus	hop
Lonicera	honeysuckle
Vitis	grape vine
Wisteria	wisteria

FRENCH LAYERING

This method solves the problem of layering plants with stiff inflexible stems. Rather than bury stems below soil level, the stem is laid on the ground and secured in place. Soil is then mounded up over it to bury all but two or three leaf nodes at the stem tip. This method can produce large numbers of young plants, and is used to propagate rootstocks of fruit trees.

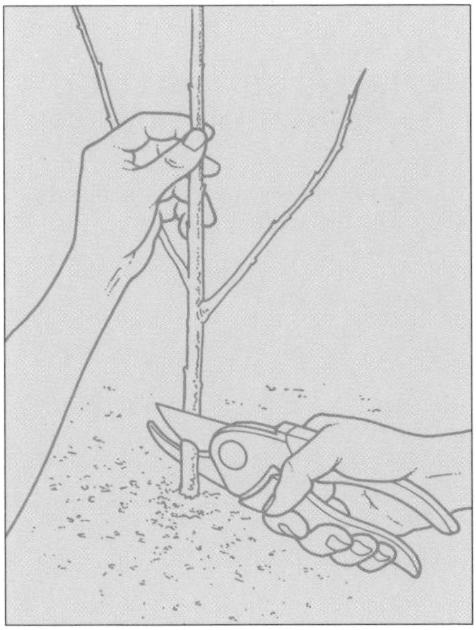

Prepare by cutting stems to the ground

Method

Choose an established plant which has been in the ground for at least two years. In spring, stool the selected plant by pruning hard, virtually to the ground, to encourage vigorous new growth.

The following spring, lightly dig over the soil surrounding the plant adding organic matter and grit to improve drainage if necessary.

Select one or several of the new stems, bend them down to the ground and carefully pin them with bent wire to hold them securely in place. Shoots will develop at the nodes. When they are about 7.5 cm (3 in) tall, mound fresh soil

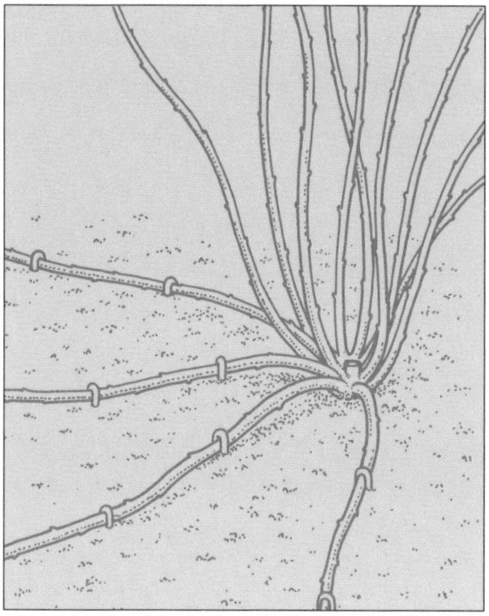

Pin new shoots down and cover with a mound of soil

over them to leave just the tips exposed. As the shoots grow taller, pile on more soil to encourage taller stems and further root formation.

Aftercare

Water well, especially during the summer, and keep the area free from weeds.

Dig around the buried stems in the following spring, taking care not to damage any root growth. Cut the exposed stems from the parent plant and between the new vertical shoots and either pot up or transplant the new plants to a sheltered bed to grow on for another season.

WHAT CAN GO WRONG

STEM ROTS IN THE SOIL

Problem: the soil has poor drainage
Action: dig in extra drainage material, such as grit or sand, into the soil below the stem before layering

PLANTS SUITABLE FOR FRENCH LAYERING

Cornus alba, C. sericea	dogwood
Cotinus coggygria	smokebush
Cydonia oblonga	quince
Malus	apple
Prunus	cherry, peach
Pyrus	pear
Salix	willow
Viburnum	viburnum

MOUND LAYERING

This is a similar method to French layering, in that the plants are prepared by stooling (cutting stems down to ground level). This method suits plants that tend to put up several shoots from the ground and can tolerate hard pruning. It is a good method for gaining a large number of new plants for rootstocks or hedging.

Method

In early spring, stool the selected plant by pruning hard, virtually to the ground, to encourage vigorous new growth. Choose established plants which have been in the ground for at least two years.

Prepare a supply of topsoil or garden soil, adding some well-rotted organic matter and possibly grit for extra drainage.

Allow the new shoots to grow to about 15 cm (6 in), then start to mound up around them with soil, leaving the top 5 cm (2 in) exposed. The shoots will form roots in the mounded soil. Continue to add soil during the summer until the mound reaches about halfway up the stems.

Aftercare

Water well, especially in warm weather, and keep the area weed free.

The following spring, carefully pull away some of the soil to expose the stems and cut the stems from the main plant below the newly formed root systems. Transplant the new plants to a sheltered site or pot up to grow on for another year before planting out.

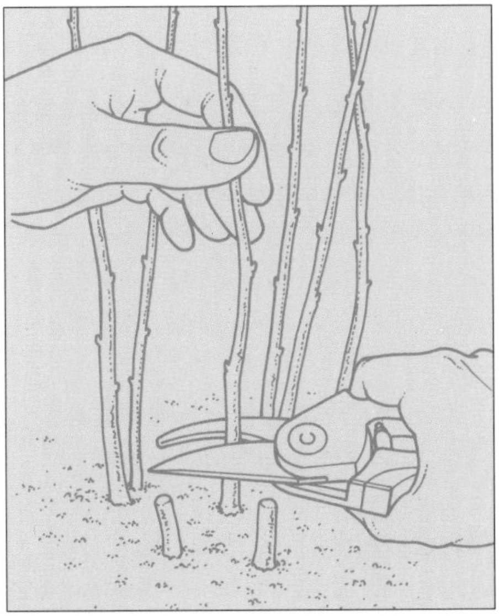

Prepare the plant by cutting the stems to ground level

Use a small trowel to mound soil over the new emerging shoots

WHAT CAN GO WRONG

THE PARENT PLANT DIES

Problem: the new shoots were covered so that the leaves couldn't continue to manufacture food for the roots

Action: remember to leave the top of the shoots uncovered when mounding the soil

PLANTS SUITABLE FOR MOUND LAYERING

Aralia	aralia
Corylus	hazel
Cydonia oblonga	quince
Deutzia	deutzia
Malus	apple
Philadelphus	mock orange
Ribes	blackcurrant, gooseberry
Rubus	blackberry, raspberry
Spiraea	spiraea

TIP LAYERING

Anyone who has ever collected blackberries or who gardens where wild blackberries grow will have seen their tendency to spread along hedges by tip layering. A long stem falls to the ground and when the shoot tip comes into contact with the soil it swells then quickly pushes out roots. Not long after, a new shoot will develop from the new root system and so the blackberry spreads.

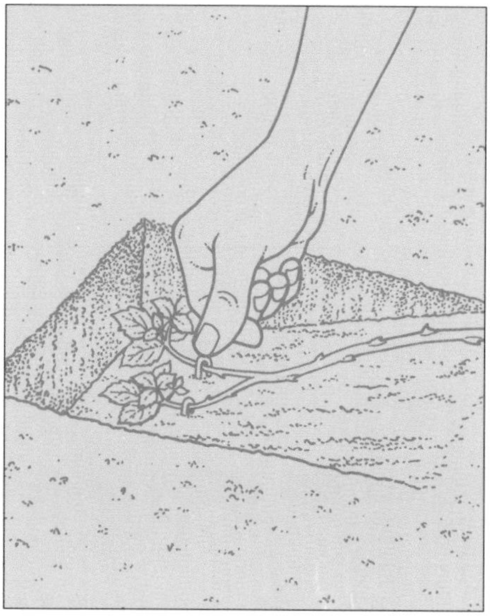

Bury the shoot tip in soil

Method

In midsummer, just dig a hole where you want to bury the stem tip. Improve the soil with organic matter and then bury the tip to about 50 cm (2 in) deep and firm gently. To hold it in place, tie the main stem to a cane inserted into the soil.

Several shoots can be buried at the same time if more plants are needed.

Aftercare

Water well, especially warm weather, and keep the area weed free.

Rooting may take only a few weeks,

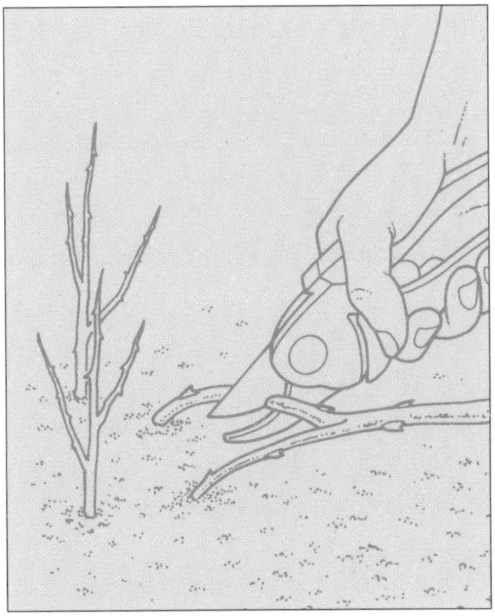

Sever the tip the following spring

PLANTS SUITABLE FOR TIP LAYERING

Forsythia	forsythia
Rubus	blackberry, raspberry

but leave the stem in situ until the following spring when the tip can be severed from the stem and potted up or planted out into the allotment or border.

AIR LAYERING

This is a slightly more unusual method of layering. Although the stem still needs to be in contact with a rooting medium, the rooting medium is brought up to the stem rather than the stem being taken down to soil level.

This method is ideal for propagating houseplants when the stems have either grown too tall for the room or the lower leaves have fallen, leaving unsightly bare stems. The layer is made on the bare stem. When it is removed after rooting, the stem of the parent plant is shortened and this often results in a more attractive, bushier parent plant.

This method can also be used on some hardy shrubs growing in pots or in the ground, but rooting may take longer in the lower outdoor temperatures.

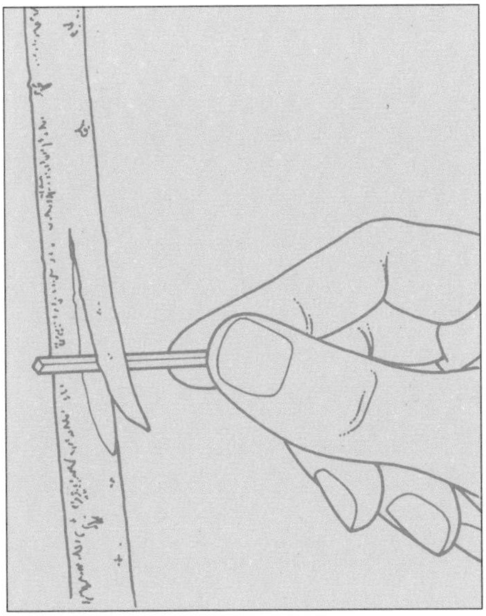

Make a shallow cut and wedge it open with a matchstick

Method for indoor plants

Ensure plants are growing strongly and healthily with no signs of pest or disease. Identify the stems of the current season's growth. Use a clean, sharp knife to make a diagonal cut 2.5–4 cm (1–1½ in) long about a third of the way into the stem. Use a matchstick to hold the slit open and apply rooting hormone to the cut surfaces.

Soak some sphagnum moss or peat in water, then squeeze out the excess. Carefully pack a small amount into the cut area. Tie a plastic bag around the stem below the cut using a garden tie to create a wide tube. Fill the bag with soaked moss or peat. Secure the top with another garden tie so that the seal is watertight and the bag is held firmly around the stem.

Aftercare of indoor plants

Keep the plant in a warm position out of direct sunlight. Ensure that the rooting medium stays moist and add more water if necessary.

Look for signs of rooting through the plastic after 6–8 weeks, depending on the temperature. Wait until the roots fill the bag before cutting the stem below the roots but just above a leaf node.

Trim off any surplus stem below the roots, then remove the plastic and gently tease out the moss or peat. Transfer to a pot that is slightly larger than the root ball using fresh compost. If there is a lot of top growth, trim back the stems to ensure the roots can sustain the new plant. Keep warm and moist.

Method for outdoor plants

Ensure plants are growing strongly and healthily with no signs of pest or disease. In spring, identify the stems of the current season's growth. Make two cuts into the bark right around the stem, about 2.5 cm (1 in) apart. Peel off the strip of bark between the cuts to expose the stem below. Apply rooting hormone to the bare stem.

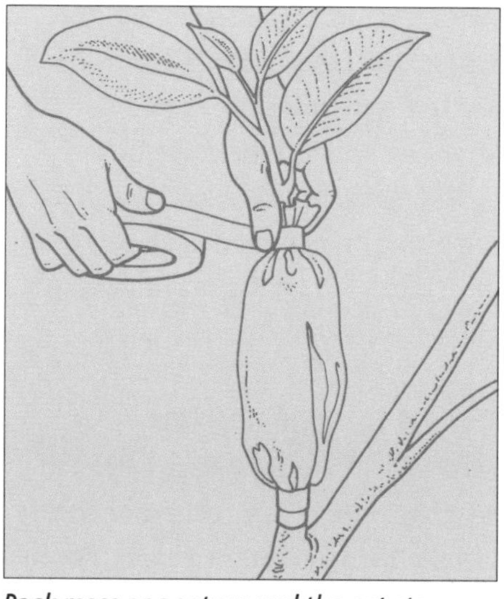

Pack moss or peat around the cut stem

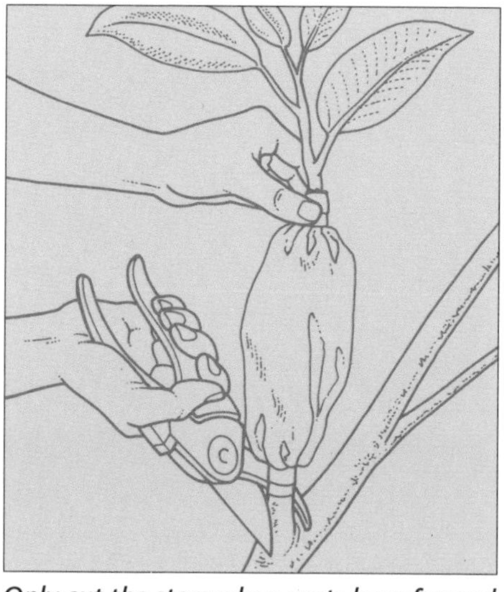

Only cut the stem when roots have formed

Camellia japonica can be propagated by air layering

PLANTS SUITABLE FOR AIR LAYERING

Indoor:	
Bougainvillea	bougainvillea
Citrus	orange, lemon
Codiaeum variegatum	croton
Dieffenbachia	dumb cane
Dracaena	dragon tree
Ficus elastica	rubber plant
Nerium oleander	oleander
Schefflera	schefflera
Outdoor:	
Camellia	camellia
Hamamelis	witch hazel
Ilex	holly
Magnolia	magnolia
Rhododendron	azalea, rhododendron

Soak some sphagnum moss or peat in water, then squeeze out the excess. Carefully pack a small amount around the cut area. Tie a sheet of black plastic around the stem below the cut using a garden tie to create a wide tube. Fill the plastic tube with more soaked sphagnum moss or peat. Secure the top with another garden tie so that the seal is watertight and the plastic is held firmly around the stem.

Aftercare of outdoor plants

Open up the plastic occasionally to check for signs of rooting. This may take up to 12 months. When the plastic is full of roots, sever the stem below the wound but just above a leaf node. Pot up the new plant in multi-purpose compost to grow on for another year. If conditions are favourable, plant out immediately, but keep well watered and protected from cold weather in the first year.

GRAFTING AND BUDDING

There is a certain mystery attached to grafting; it's an age-old craft which has been practised by skilled gardeners since ancient times. It does require skill as this is not a propagation technique where you can just stick a seed or stem in the soil and see what happens. That said, once the principles of grafting are understood then it is much easier to unravel the mystery and have a go.

Fruit trees are propagated using grafting techniques

Budding and grafting are two techniques whereby a piece of one plant is taken and placed on another plant in such a way that the two pieces fuse together and grow thereafter as one plant. In grafting, a piece of stem is cut in such a way as to fit closely onto the stem of the rootstock, but in budding it is only the area immediately around a dormant bud that is used. Both techniques have their advantages and have been found to be successful for certain plants. Through time, several different methods of trimming and joining the stem (scion) and rootstock have been developed, with some requiring more skill with a knife than others.

These techniques are only used on perennial plants with a permanent stem structure such as trees, conifers, shrubs and woody climbers. Propagation techniques such as cuttings and division only require a piece of the desired plant to be taken and encouraged to grow for itself. Budding and grafting, however, are more complicated methods as they require another established plant to provide the roots and stem from which the new plant will grow. The process requires more preparation in finding a plant to act as the root (rootstock) but also some careful practice in trimming both this and the piece of plant that will be attached to it, whether it be bud or stem (scion). The matching of scion to rootstock is called the union and is key to the success of the technique.

Stem structure and grafting

There is an area under the bark encircling woody stems where plant cells have the capacity to divide and increase in number. This layer of active cells is called the cambium and it is often visible as a faint line below the bark. If two cut surfaces exposing these cambium cells are brought together, the tendency to divide can be activated and the cells proliferate, forming a callus and sealing the join. Then, incredibly, the cells can change, forming extra vessels to move water or food around the plant and into the new portion so that it becomes connected to the main body of the plant.

The remaining top growth of the old plant is cut away so that the roots support only the new section. The new section grows and develops, retaining its own unique

This prunus graft shows clearly the scion and rootstock, with wound sealant and support

characteristics, while the section below the union also retains its identity. So a plant formed by budding or grafting has the rootstock of one plant and the stems and leaves of another, although they function as one when moving food and water around the plant.

A simple graft will sometimes happen naturally between two stems on the same plant where they have rubbed together, so removing the bark and causing them to fuse. For grafting or budding to be successful, the two plants need to be closely related. They are often of the same species, but can be within the same genus or perhaps the same family.

ADVANTAGES OF GRAFTING

- There are plants where propagation by cuttings is not very successful, but budding or grafting gives a better rate of success.
- Once successful, the new plant already has an established root system and so requires little extra care to grow into an established plant more quickly.
- Budding uses a small amount of propagation material so it can be used to propagate cultivars in larger numbers than would often be possible by cuttings.
- The rootstock can be chosen to confer extra attributes onto the plant being propagated. For example, it may be less prone to soil-borne diseases, less likely to produce suckers, or confer extra vigour. Where fruit trees are grafted, the desired fruit variety can be grafted onto a choice of rootstock to control the ultimate size of the tree, making it better suited to a small garden. Using dwarf rootstock has also been found to bring fruit trees into flower and fruit at a younger age, a useful attribute for the impatient gardener.
- The technique can be used to manipulate plants for extra horticultural value. For example, a 'family' apple tree has two or more varieties grafted onto a single stem. Shrubs with low horizontal growth can be grafted onto a tall straight stem to create a small weeping ‘tree’.

Basic guidelines for successful grafting

- **The knife** Invest in a specialized grafting and budding knife and keep it clean at all times. Always keep the knife sharp as this makes it easier to control and will result in a cleaner cut. If you are worried about cutting yourself, a useful tip is to protect vulnerable thumbs with a plaster or tape.
- **Practice** Use spare prunings from the garden to practise making the correct cuts for the chosen technique. Push older stems into the ground to act as the rootstock.
- **Selecting rootstocks** Select a compatible rootstock and acquire more material than is actually required, to allow for losses. This can be bought from a grower or produced economically by propagating appropriate material by mound layering (see page 95), French layering (see page 93) or occasionally by seed. The rootstocks need to be about two years old with a length of clear straight stem 15–45 cm (6–18 in) above soil level, depending on the technique to be used.
- **Selecting scions** Use scion wood that is the current season's growth as the potential for cell proliferation at the cambium layer is high. The ability tails off as the wood matures.
- **Matching rootstock to scion** When making the graft, check that the cambium layer on both scion and rootstock match up before they are secured together.
- **Work quickly** Seal the union immediately to prevent it drying out before the callus has formed.

EQUIPMENT

As with other methods of propagation, having the correct tools and equipment usually leads to a greater chance of success.

- **Secateurs** These are required for taking scion material from the parent plant and can be used to trim the rootstock. Ensure that they are clean and sharp.
- **Sharp knife** A specialist straight-bladed knife is used to trim stems for grafting. A specially designed budding knife has a curved spatula blade which is used to lift the bark when T-budding. A blade that folds away into a wooden or plastic handle is safer. Ensure the blade is clean and sharp.
- **Grafting tape** This is a clear polythene tape used to bind the scion and rootstock together until the callus forms. It can be stretched gently to cover the union completely to prevent drying out. A medium grade food bag cut into a long strip may serve as an alternative.
- **Binding material** Raffia soaked in water or cut elastic bands can be wound tightly around the stem to secure the scion and rootstock.
- **Budding patches** These small rubber patches with hooks are used to bind bud grafts when T-budding roses.

- **Grafting wax** This can be applied to seal the graft union and prevent drying out while the callus is forming.
- **Large polythene bags** For small plants with limited top growth, a plastic bag can be used to cover the whole plant to reduce water loss.
- **Heated greenhouse** Although bottom heat isn't required for root formation, a raised temperature can aid cell division and so speed the formation of the callus at the union.

WHIP AND TONGUE GRAFT

This technique is most often used on fruit trees and some ornamental plants during the winter or early spring before the buds start to swell. Plant a one-year-old rootstock in spring where it is to grow, or in a nursery bed if you have plenty to spare. The graft can then be made the following year, by which time the root system will be well established in the ground. This technique is suitable where both rootstock and scion are approximately the same girth and no more than 2.5 cm (1 in) thick. Part of the scion is left exposed, so the technique works better when the growing environment is damp, preventing it drying out.

Selecting scions

Collect suitable scion wood in midwinter – this could be stems cut during routine winter pruning. Select healthy, vigorous, ripened wood of the previous season's growth. The stems should be about pencil thickness and straight as they will form the trunk. Use secateurs to cut each length to about 23 cm (9 in), making the cut just above a bud to avoid any snags. Take more than you require to allow for spares.

Place the scion wood in a plastic bag in the refrigerator, or bury it diagonally in sand to leave one end just exposed. Leave in place until early spring.

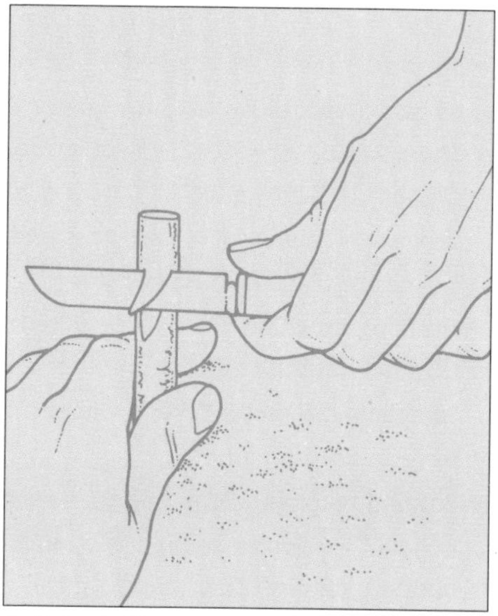

Pull the knife upwards in a sloping cut

Preparing the rootstock

In early spring, use secateurs to cut horizontally across the rootstock 15–30 cm (6–12 in) above soil level. Bend over the remaining stem and prepare to cut a section off the top. Start with the blade of the grafting knife about 4 cm (1½ in) below the top and then draw the knife upwards to make a sloping cut and remove a slice. Make a 0.5 cm (1/4 in) deep cut down into the exposed face, starting just below the top. The resulting flap is called the 'tongue'.

Preparing the scion

To prepare the scion, use secateurs to remove the soft tip, then trim the scion down to four buds, making the cut about 4 cm (1 1/2 in) below the lower bud. Next use the knife to make a slanting cut down the stem on the opposite side to the lower bud, cutting from the bud to the base.

Put the scion stem against the rootstock with the sloping cuts flush to see how the two match up. Note where the tongue on the rootstock sits, then make a corresponding vertical cut in the scion so that the tongues can interlock, holding the scion in place.

Making the graft

Adjust the stems so that the cambium layers match, preferably on both sides. Ideally, the cut faces of the two stems should match so that no tissue is left exposed.

Take a length of grafting tape and tie a half hitch around the stem about 5 cm (2 in) below the graft. Tension the tape so that it stretches slightly and then wind it firmly around the stem and over the graft, taking care not to dislodge the scion. Continue to cover any exposed stem and secure with another tight half hitch about 5 cm (2 in) above the graft.

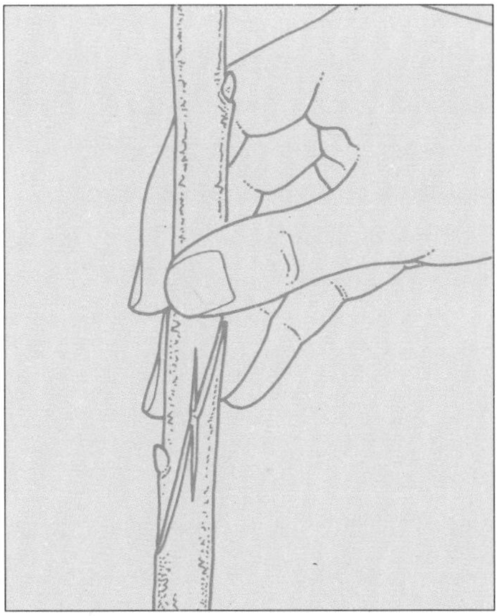

Interlock the two tongues to hold in place

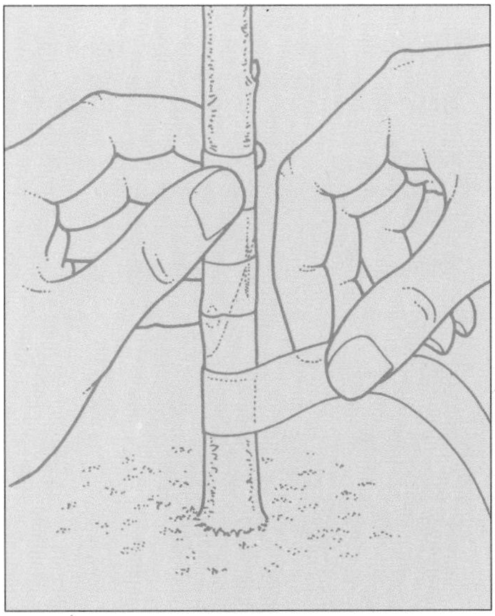

Tightly bind the graft with clear tape

WHAT CAN GO WRONG

THE GRAFT DOESN'T TAKE

Problem: air entered the graft union and the surfaces dried out
Action: tie the tape firmly so that the two pieces are in close contact. Practise the tying on spare pieces of wood

Problem: disease has entered the graft union
Action: avoid touching the cut surfaces of the scion or rootstock

Problem: there was a difference in the size of the scion and rootstock stems
Action: select stems of a similar size or make the cut in the rootstock more shallow to match that of the scion

PLANTS SUITABLE FOR WHIP AND TONGUE GRAFT

Daphne	daphne
Fraxinus	ash
Juglans	walnut
Malus	apple
Prunus	cherry, peach
Pyrus	pear
Salix caprea	goat willow

Aftercare

Check for signs of callusing after about six weeks. It will show as a brown seal between the cut layers. Remove the grafting tape to allow the scion buds to break. Choose the strongest (usually the uppermost) to grow on to form the tree and tie the shoot to a cane to keep it straight. Cut off the other shoots once they are 3–4 leaves long. Rub off any shoots that form on the rootstock.

SIDE GRAFT

This technique is used when the stem of the rootstock is thicker than that of the scion and is usually carried out on container-grown plants in late winter or early spring. This is a useful technique if border space is at a premium but you have a cool greenhouse for overnight protection in winter.

Selecting scions

Collect suitable scion wood in midwinter, selecting healthy, vigorous, ripened wood of the previous season's growth. Use secateurs to cut a two-year-old stem just above a bud, but include the tip of growth made in the previous year.

Store the scion wood until early spring in a plastic bag in the refrigerator.

Preparing the rootstock

In early spring, collect together healthy two-year-old compatible plants, choosing those with straight stems and a good root system so that they can support the scion well. Place them in a cool greenhouse with a night temperature of 7–10°C (46–50°F) for two weeks before grafting.

To prepare the rootstock, use secateurs to cut horizontally across the stem 7.5–10 cm (3–4 in) above soil level. Use the grafting knife to make a short sloping cut down into the stem on one side, about 2.5 cm (1 in) from the top. Now cut down to remove a sliver of stem to meet the first cut. This should leave the rootstock stem with a flat face with an angled ledge at the base.

Preparing the scion

To prepare the scion, use secateurs to remove the soft tip and trim the stem to 15–25 cm (6–10 in) long. Also make a fresh cut across the base. Use the knife to make a shallow slanting cut across the stem on the opposite side to the lower bud, cutting from the bud to the base. Then make a short angled cut on the base to mirror that on the stock.

Making the graft

Position the scion stem against the stock so that it sits in the lower ledge. The two cut surfaces and the cambium layers should match completely so that no tissue is left exposed. It is better to make a smaller cut in the stock and then make it bigger to match the scion than to make the cut too deep initially so that tissue is exposed that the scion won't cover.

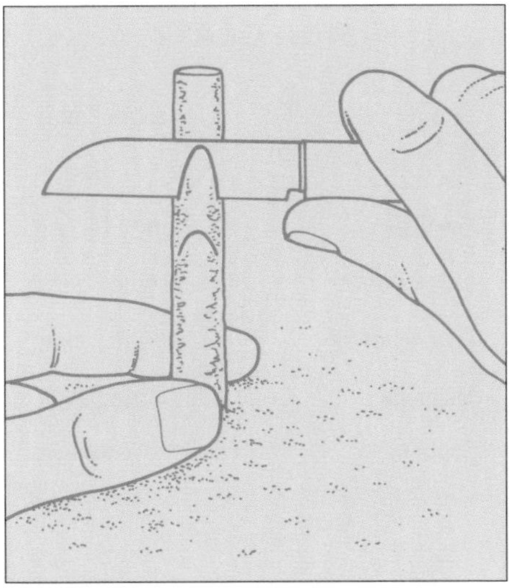

Remove a sliver of stem from the stock

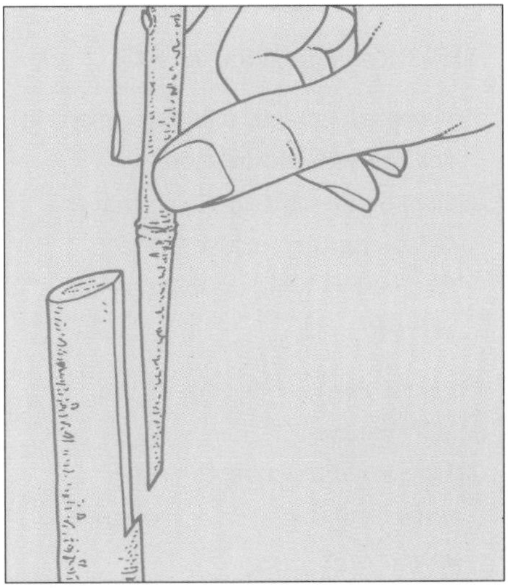

Position the scion against the rootstock

Take a length of grafting tape and tie a half hitch around the stem about 5 cm (2 in) below the graft. Tension the tape and then wind it firmly around the stem and over the graft union, taking care not to dislodge the two stems. Continue to cover the exposed stems and secure with another tight half hitch about 5 cm (2 in) above the graft.

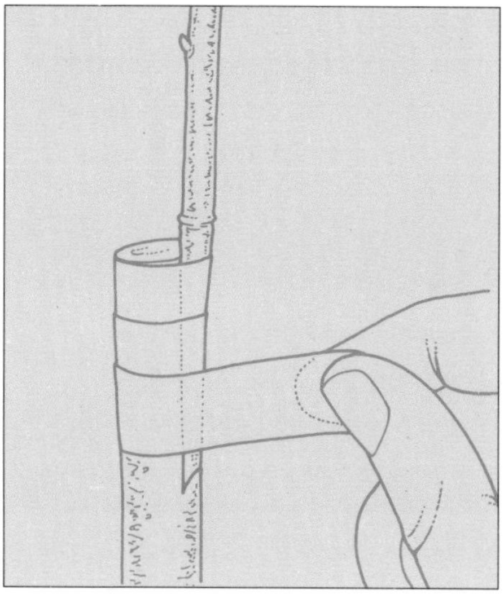

Bind tightly with clear tape

Aftercare

Maintain plants at the same temperature and keep them shaded from direct sun. Check for signs of callusing after about six weeks. It will show as a pale seal between the cut layers, turning brown as it matures.

Remove the grafting tape to allow the scion buds to break. Transfer to a cold frame and grow on before planting out in autumn or the following spring. Remove any shoots that grow from the stock.

WHAT CAN GO WRONG

THE GRAFT DOESN'T TAKE

Problem: air entered the graft union and the surfaces dried out
Action: tie the tape firmly so that the two pieces are in close contact. Practise the tying on spare pieces of wood

Problem: disease has entered the graft union
Action: avoid touching the cut surfaces of the scion or rootstock as you work

PLANTS SUITABLE FOR SIDE GRAFT

Betula	silver birch
Fagus	beech
Gleditsia	honey locust
Liquidambar	sweet gum
Liviodendron	tulip tree
Magnolia	magnolia
Sophera	sophora

SPLICED SIDE-VENEER GRAFT

This technique is very similar to side grafting, but the top growth of the rootstock isn't trimmed off until the graft has taken and the callus has formed. The graft is made in late winter or in summer, depending on the plant. In summer the top growth helps to maintain the flow of sap to the union which helps the callus to form. It is most often used on conifers and shrubs or trees with a thin bark.

If you are planning to graft deciduous plants in winter, follow the instructions for side grafting on the previous pages. If you are grafting evergreens, or are working in summer, follow the instructions below.

Selecting scions

Collect suitable scion wood from healthy vigorous stems of the current season's growth. Use secateurs to cut the stem just above a bud to give a scion length of about 15 cm (6 in). Store the scion wood in a plastic bag to prevent it drying out.

Preparing the rootstock

Choose healthy two-year-old compatible plants with straight stems and a good root system so that they can support the scion well. Trim off the lower branches.

Use a knife to make a short cut at 45° down into one side of the stem about 5–7.5 cm (2–3 in) from the base, away from any dormant buds.

Hold the scion up against the stock to check the width of cut needed to match them correctly. Starting about 2.5 cm (1 in) above your first cut, gently cut down into the stock stem to remove a sliver of stem to meet the first cut. This should leave the stock with a flat face with an angled ledge at the base.

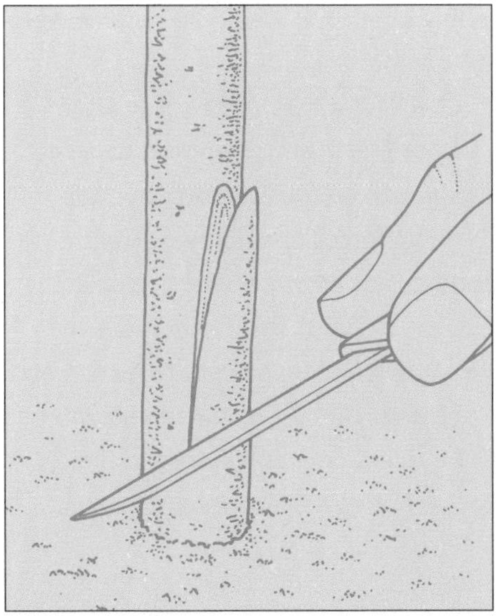

Remove a piece of stem low to the ground

Preparing the scion

To prepare the scion, remove the lower leaves to expose the stem and draw the knife down to make a shallow slanting cut about 2.5 cm (1 in) long across the base of the stem. Then make a short angled cut on the base to mirror that on the stock.

Making the graft

Position the scion stem against the stock so that it sits in the lower ledge. The two cut surfaces and the cambium layers should match completely so that no tissue is left exposed. Secure the cut surfaces together using raffia or lengths of elastic band.

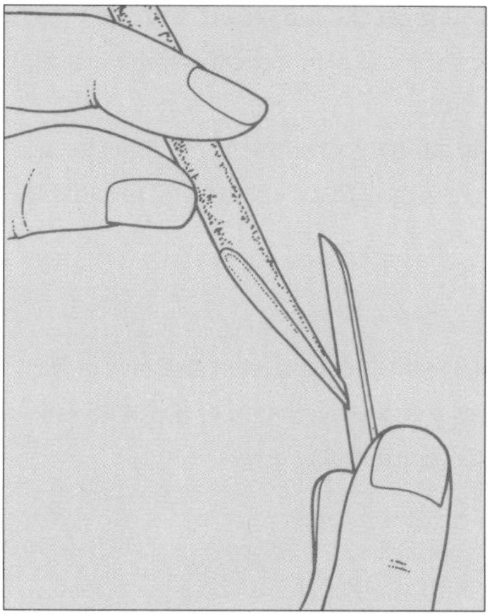

Trim the scion to match the cut surfaces

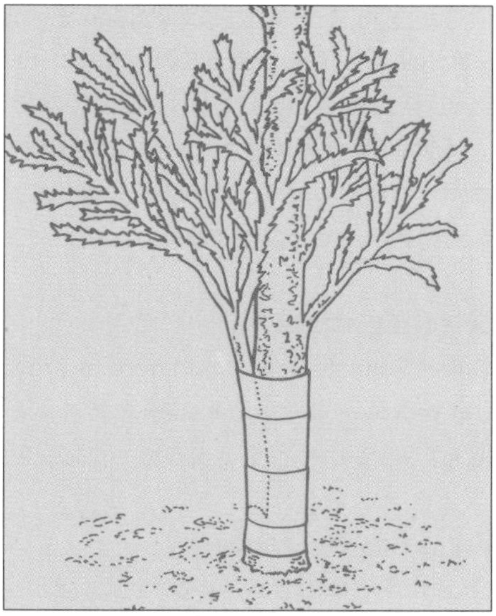

Secure the two pieces together

PLANTS SUITABLE FOR SPLICED SIDE-VENEER GRAFT

Acer palmatum	Japanese acer
Chamaecyparis	cypress
Daphne	daphne
Gleditsia	honey locust
Liquidambar	sweet gum
Magnolia	magnolia
Pinus	pine
Rhododendron	rhododendron

Aftercare

Place the plants in a humid environment, at about 15°C (59°F), to aid callus formation. A heated bench covered with a polythene tent or a heated propagator with a high cover would be suitable. Keep the compost moist.

Check for a thin white callus after three or four weeks, then trim back the top growth on the rootstock by half. Once the callus turns brown after another two or three weeks, remove the binding. Begin to steadily increase the ventilation and then begin to harden off.

Remove the rest of the top growth on the rootstock after another six weeks or so once the plants are acclimatized to their normal growing conditions. Keep the plants protected but cool over winter and plant out the following spring.

WHAT CAN GO WRONG	
THE GRAFT DOESN'T TAKE	**THE SCION DIES**
Problem: the callus isn't fully developed before the remaining top growth on the rootstock is removed **Action:** be sure to wait until the callus is fully formed and the plant hardened off before removing the remaining top growth **Problem:** air entered the graft union and the surfaces dried out **Action:** tie the tape firmly so that the two pieces are in close contact. Practise the tying on spare pieces of wood **Problem:** disease has entered the graft union **Action:** avoid touching the cut surfaces of the scion or rootstock	**Problem:** the grafted plant is kept too warm and the scion continues to grow **Action:** keep the temperature at 15°C (59°F) and make sure the compost is just barely moist **Problem:** the scion loses too much moisture from its leaves **Action:** maintain a humid environment around the graft until the callused area is brown

APICAL WEDGE GRAFT

This is a useful method for propagating most shrubs and climbers and is particularly useful for cultivars that don't readily root from cuttings or those, like wisteria, which are weak and slow to flower when raised from seed. It is generally carried out on containerized plants in summer, but it can be used on hardy outdoor plants in winter. The technique involves placing the scion stem into a wedge cut in the rootstock. For greater success, the two stems should be the same diameter, but the position of the scion on the stock can be manipulated to achieve a good match of cambium.

The rootstock must be compatible, preferably the species form of the cultivar to be grafted. The rootstock could be grown from a cutting or raised from seed.

Selecting and preparing the scions

In summer, collect suitable scion wood from healthy vigorous stems of the current season's growth (ideally pencil thickness). Use secateurs to cut the stem just above a bud to give a scion length of 7.5–12.5 cm (3–5 in), with two to four buds present. Store the scion wood in a plastic bag to prevent it drying out.

Use a clean, sharp grafting knife to cut the base of the scion to create a sharp edge.

First make a slanting cut from about 2.5 cm (1 in) above the base downwards to the centre of the stem. Repeat on the opposite side of the stem to create tapering point at the base.

Preparing the rootstocks

Select compatible rootstocks. These will be ready to use when the stem is about pencil thick, which could be in the season following propagation for vigorous plants. Keep the compost just moist for two weeks prior to grafting to reduce sap flow.

To prepare the stock, cut across the main stem just above the roots. Make sure that the cut is clean, trimming it if necessary to make it smooth.

Making the graft

Make a vertical slit in the rootstock slightly shorter in depth than the point of the trimmed scion. If both scion and stock are of the same diameter, make the slit in the centre of the stock. However, if the stock is bigger than the scion, make the cut towards one side so that the point on the scion is the same width as the cut in the stock. In this way, the cambium layer just under the bark should match up on both sides.

Push the scion right down into the slit in the stock so that only a small area is left exposed.

Secure in position with polythene grafting tape or a cut elastic band, then seal the area with clingfilm. With this technique, the tape doesn't need to be stretched taut before tying.

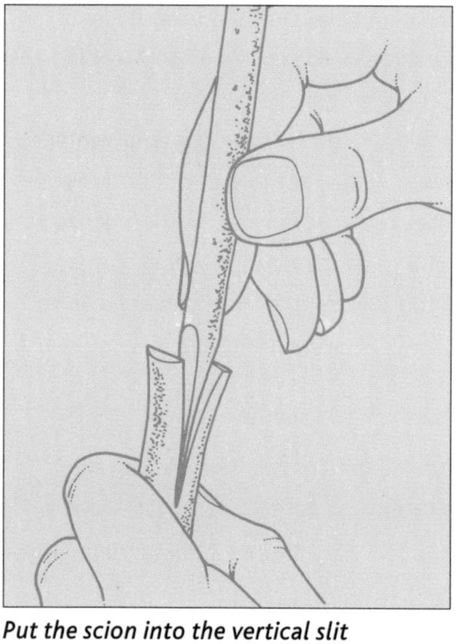

Put the scion into the vertical slit

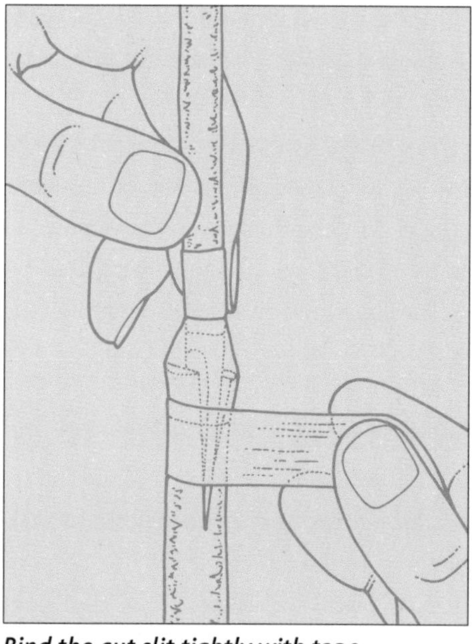

Bind the cut slit tightly with tape

WHAT CAN GO WRONG

THE GRAFT DOESN'T TAKE

Problem: the cut surfaces weren't in close contact and dried out
Action: practise making the cuts so that the surface is flat, to get good contact. Draw the two surfaces together when binding to ensure good contact

Problem: the stems were different sizes so there was not enough contact between cambium layers
Action: be sure to make the cut in the stock the same size as the scion. If the scion stem is smaller and the cut in the stock is too long, place the scion up to the edge of the stock so the cambium matches on one side of both stock and scion

Problem: the graft area is flooded with sap
Action: water the plants sparingly before making the graft and during the period of aftercare. Only increase watering when giving extra ventilation

Laburnum is suitable for apical wedge grafting

PLANTS SUITABLE FOR APICAL WEDGE GRAFT

Cercis	judas tree
Daphne	daphne
Hamamelis	witch hazel
Laburnum	golden rain
Rhododendron	rhododendron, azalea
Robinia	false acacia
Syringa	lilac

Aftercare

Place the plants in a humid environment at 15–20°C (59–68°F) to aid callus formation. A heated bench covered with a polythene tent or a heated propagator with a high cover would be suitable. Keep the compost just moist, as overwatering may cause failure.

Check for a thin white callus after three or four weeks; it will appear on the exposed cut surfaces and where the stock meets the scion. Once the callus turns brown after another two or three weeks, remove the binding.

Begin to increase the ventilation steadily by opening the tent or propagator for short periods, gradually increasing the length of time. Gently harden off plants to lower temperatures but keep protected, perhaps in a cold frame, over winter. Plant outdoors in the following spring.

WHIP GRAFT

This is a variation on the apical wedge graft but definitely requires the two stems to be of the same diameter. Both the scion and stock are trimmed with a slanting cut of the same depth and angle so that when placed together they make a perfect match.

Method

Follow the general method for making an apical wedge graft (see page 111), with the following changes:

- Trim the rootstock stem to about 10–12.5 cm (4–5 in) above the roots.
- Make an angled cut across the top of the stock.
- Trim the scion to 7.5–10 cm (3–4 in) long, cutting preferably below a bud.
- Make a slanting cut in the scion to mirror that of the stock, starting on the side opposite the lower bud.
- Bind the two surfaces firmly together using polythene grafting tape.

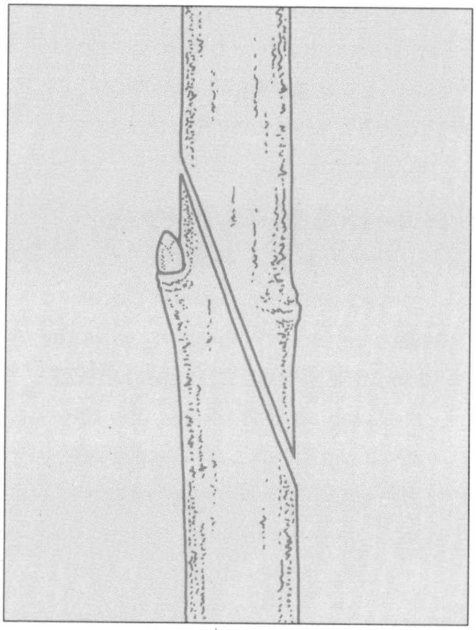

A simple whip graft

Treat the graft plant in the same way as for an apical wedge graft (see page 111).

CHIP BUDDING

This is a popular method used commercially to graft fruit tree cultivars onto a chosen rootstock. The method requires little material, using only a single bud on a short piece of stem as the scion. It is a useful and successful method for gardeners too but, as with all grafting, a little practise at making the cuts will improve the chances of success.

Some planning and preparation is needed as compatible one-year-old rootstocks should be ordered and planted out in a nursery bed or their final positions the previous year. If budding fails, it is common practise to wait until the following year, then cut the rootstock lower to the ground and make a whip and tongue graft instead (see page 104).

Selecting bud sticks

Collect bud sticks from a healthy plant in mid to late summer. Select well-ripened stems of pencil thickness that are turning brown at the base, usually from the sunny side of the plant.

Remove all the leaves with a sharp knife but leave a short amount of leaf stalk. Place the bud sticks in a bucket of water to stop them drying out.

Preparing the rootstock

The two-year-old compatible rootstock should have been planted out in spring. Prepare it by removing all leaves from the bottom 30 cm (12 in) of stem.

Stand over the plant and select an area of smooth stem, preferably on the shady side and 15–30 cm (6–12 in) above the ground. Use a clean sharp grafting knife to make a short angled cut into the stem just above a leaf node. Then remove a sliver of bark about 4 cm (1½ in) long by cutting downwards towards the first cut.

Preparing the bud

Prepare the bud by making a short angled cut into the stem just below a chosen bud. Make another cut, starting about 4 cm (1½ in) above the first and pulling the knife towards the first cut as it slices behind the leaf bud and removes it from the stem. Disregard any rounded fruit buds, selecting only the pointed leaf buds. Detach the piece of bud material by holding the leaf stalk so that you don't touch the cambium layer.

Making the graft

Match up the bud to the trimmed rootstock, resting it on the angled shelf. The bud and stock should match up perfectly; practising both cuts will help achieve a good match. If the cut on the stock is too wide, place the bud to one side so that the cambium layer matches up on one side at least.

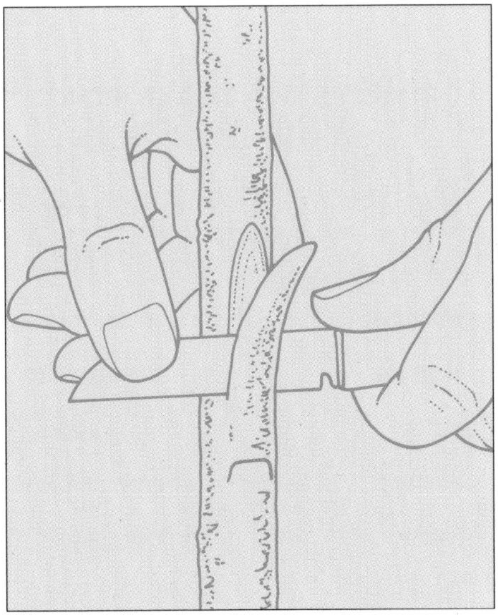

Remove a sliver from the rootstock

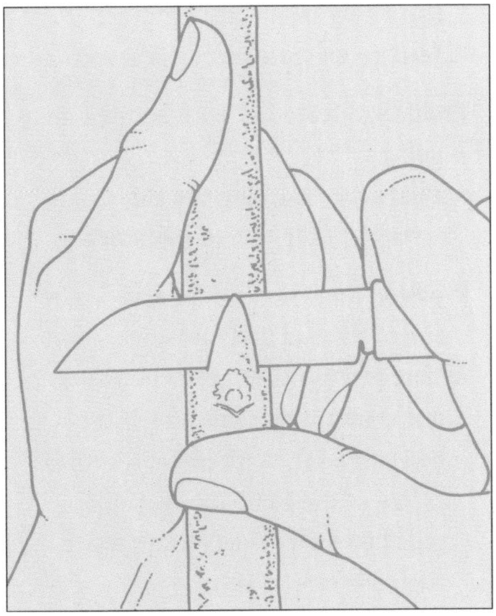

Cut a matching sliver from the scion

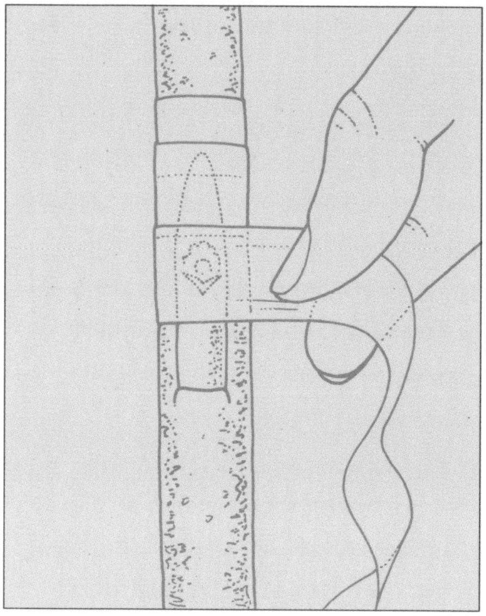

Bind the graft tightly with tape

Take a length of grafting tape and tie a half hitch around the stem about 5 cm (2 in) below the bud. Tension the tape so that it stretches slightly and then wind it firmly around the stem and over the bud, taking care not to dislodge it. Continue to wind and secure with another tight half hitch 5 cm (2 in) above the graft.

Aftercare

Check for callus formation, a brown seal between bud and stem, after six or eight weeks. The bud should still be plump, not shrivelled. Remove the grafting tape and leave the plant over winter.

The following spring, as the buds on the rootstock begin to burst, use secateurs to cut back the stem to just above the budded portion. Remove any shoots below the budded section when they are about 10 cm (4 in) long.

Only tie the shoot to a cane if it doesn't grow upright. Train the tree by formative pruning the following spring.

WHAT CAN GO WRONG

THE BUD DOESN'T TAKE

Problem: air entered the bud union and the surfaces dried out

Action: tie the tape firmly so that the two pieces are in close contact. Practise on spare pieces of wood

Problem: disease has entered the bud union

Action: avoid touching the cut surfaces of the bud or rootstock

Problem: there was a difference in the size of the bud and rootstock stems

Action: practise cutting the bud stick and stem to the same size. If the bud is smaller, don't place it in the centre as the cambium may not touch on either side. Always try to align one side at least

PLANTS SUITABLE FOR WHIP GRAFT

Citrus	lemon
Ilex	holly
Laburnum	golden rain
Magnolia	magnolia
Malus	apple
Prunus	cherry, peach
Sorbus	mountain ash
Ulmus	elm

T-BUDDING ROSES

This technique is perhaps more difficult than chip budding in terms of achieving a successful union between the stock and the scion bud. It is frequently used for roses, but is also suitable for trees. Like chip budding, a single leaf bud is removed from the stem of the scion but the woody stem remnants behind the bud are removed as well, exposing the complete cambium layer sitting just under the bark and bud. This small piece of material is slipped under the bark of the rootstock so the exposed area of cambium is much larger. The bark is cut in a T shape and then eased open to accept the bud, hence the name.

Rosa canina can be used as a rootstock

The success of the technique is partly dependent on how easily the bark can be lifted away from the stem to accept the bud. Roses generally don't pose too much of a problem but some plants are more difficult, especially in drought conditions, so keep plants well watered prior to T-budding. However, the method can still fail after the bud is in place as once the wood fraction is removed from the bud it is more vulnerable to fungal disease, especially when tucked behind the bark.

There are a number of suitable rootstocks for roses, mainly species varieties such as *R. canina*, *R. laxa* and *R. multiflora*. These can be raised from seed or by cuttings, but it is best to contact specialist rose growers for availability and advice on the best selection.

Selecting bud sticks

Collect bud sticks from a healthy plant in mid to late summer. Select well-ripened stems of pencil thickness that are turning brown at the base, usually from the sunny side of the plant.

Remove all the leaves with a sharp knife but leave a short amount of leaf stalk. Wrap the bud sticks in moist newspaper to stop them drying out.

Preparing the root stock

The two-year-old compatible rootstocks should have been planted out in spring and soil earthed-up to the base of the stems.

Prepare the rootstock by removing the soil from the neck of the plant and wiping it clean of soil and grit with a dry cloth.

Use a sharp, clean budding knife to make a 0.5 cm (¼ in) cut across the stem about 2.5 cm (1 in) below the top growth. Make another vertical cut upwards to join the first and make the T. Use the spatula part of the blade to lever and prise the bark gently away from the stem to create two flaps.

Preparing the bud

Prepare the bud immediately by firstly snapping any prickles off the bud stick. Make a scooping cut behind the bud starting 0.5 cm (¼ in) above it and ending 2.5 cm (1 in) below it to make a tail.

Hold the tail and gently flex it back to release the woody portion of the stem and discard. Then cut off the tail just below the bud, taking care not to touch the exposed cambium under the bark.

Making the graft

Holding onto the leaf stalk, slide the bud down into the T cut in the stock so that the bud sits neatly between the two bark flaps. Trim the top of the bud to the horizontal cut if necessary.

Secure the bud with a rubber grafting patch, keeping the pins on the opposite side of the stem from the bud.

Aftercare

Check for callus formation after three or four weeks. The rubber patch will rot away and fall off after a few more weeks.

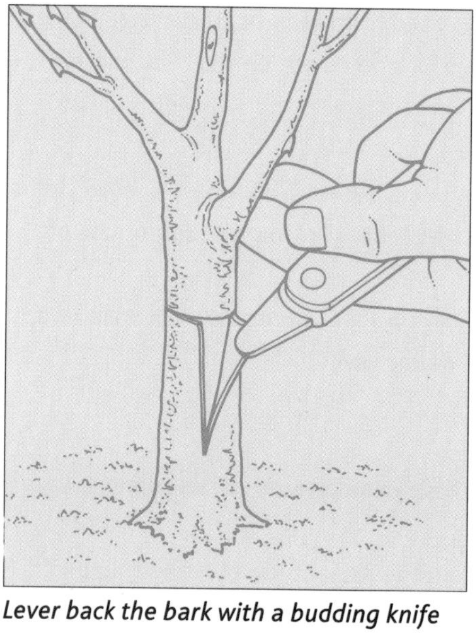

Lever back the bark with a budding knife

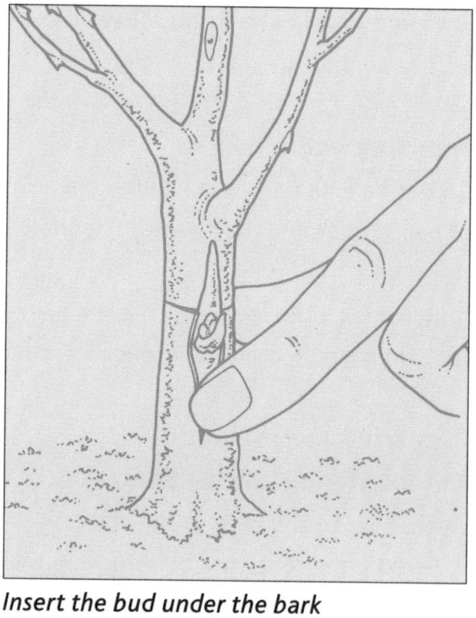

Insert the bud under the bark

The following spring, use sharp secateurs to cut back the top growth just above the dormant bud. As the bud shoots, prune it back in summer to encourage a bushier habit.

T-budding trees

Follow the instructions in the chip budding section for preparing the rootstock and bud sticks (see page 114).

Follow the instructions in the T-budding roses section for making a T cut in the stock stem, preparing the bud scion and making the graft (see page 118).

Bind the graft using plastic grafting tape, as described for chip budding (see page 116).

Check for callus formation after about six weeks, then remove the tape. Thereafter treat the tree in the same way as a chip-budded tree (see page 116).

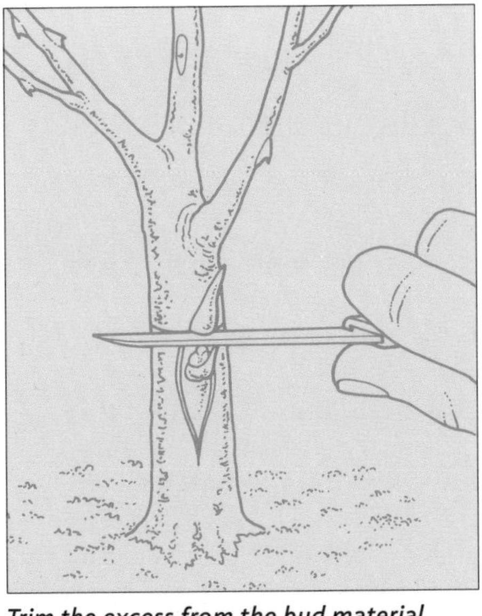

Trim the excess from the bud material

WHAT CAN GO WRONG

THE BUD DOESN'T TAKE

Problem: disease has entered the bud union

Action: avoid touching the cut surfaces of the scion or rootstock. Practise making the correct cuts on the stem and handling the bud without touching its face on rose prunings

Problem: not all the woody tissue was removed from behind the bud

Action: practise removing the woody tissue. Try scraping away any remainder with the knife

Problem: the cut surfaces dried out

Action: practise until you are proficient at completing the technique, from making the T cut to inserting the scion bud, as quickly as possible

BULBS

The term 'bulb' is used by gardeners to describe a range of plants that shoot from a swollen underground structure that serves as a food store. These plants usually show a period of dormancy after flowering. True bulbs have layers of scale leaves where food is stored arranged around the central growing shoot. In some bulbs such as alliums, narcissus and tulips, the scale leaves are tightly packed; in others, including lilies, they are arranged more loosely. Corms are slightly different in structure from bulbs, and include plants such as crocus and gladiolus. In corms, it is the stem that is the swollen food store. Also included under the general term of 'bulbs' are plants with swollen roots and stems known as tubers, and certain plants with swollen rhizomes that show a dormant season.

Propagation options

Bulbs can be grown from seed collected after flowering. The resulting plants are slow to develop and it can be upwards of four years after sowing before the plant has matured enough to flower. The seedling bulbs will also have slightly variable characteristics in relation to the parent if they have been open pollinated by bees or other pollinators.

Vegetative propagation of bulbs is a more reliable method of gaining plants identical to the parent which attain flowering size more quickly. The easiest method is by division of offsets, where new small bulbs and corms produced by the parent plant are detached and grown on (see page 86). Another easy method already discussed is to cut rhizomes and tubers, such as dahlias or begonias, into sections with each piece having one or several growing shoots (see page 83). However, there are other techniques which apply solely to bulbs and bulbous plants.

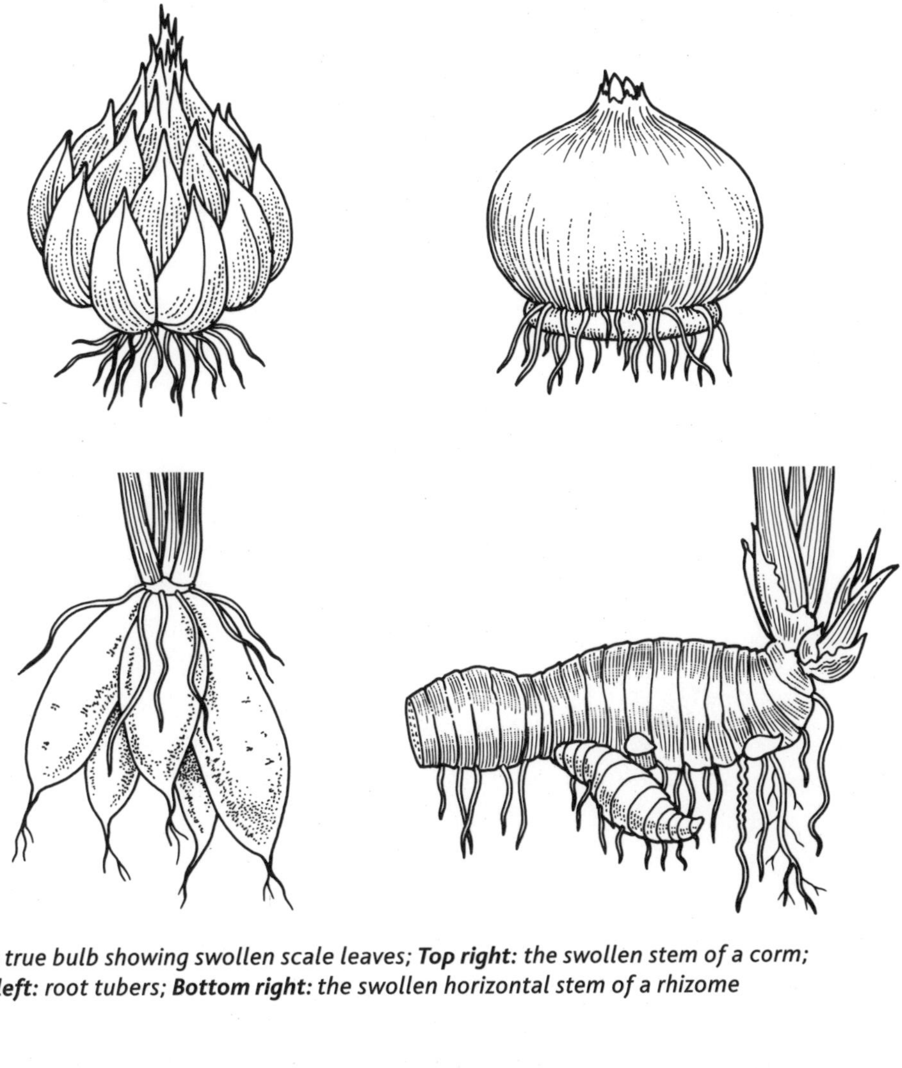

Top left: *true bulb showing swollen scale leaves;* ***Top right:*** *the swollen stem of a corm;* ***Bottom left:*** *root tubers;* ***Bottom right:*** *the swollen horizontal stem of a rhizome*

SCALING

Scaling works only with true bulbs and involves cutting the bulbs into sections, each consisting of an individual scale leaf or several scale leaves attached to a section of basal plate, the point at which roots emerge from the bulb structure. These sections are kept in warm, moist conditions to encourage rooting. Bulbous plants are very prone to fungal rots so attention to hygiene is important.

WARNING

You may wish to wear gloves to protect your skin from bulb sap and fungicide treatments when carrying out any of these techniques.

Scaling is often used for lilies (*Lilium*) and some fritillaries (*Fritillaria*) where the scale leaves are loosely packed around the bulb. It is carried out when the bulb is dormant, usually in autumn or winter. It is a useful method of increasing the numbers of bulbs already in the garden, but it can also be used on newly purchased bulbs prior to planting.

Method

Brush any soil off the bulbs and inspect them for signs of ill health, discarding any which show disease.

Snap off the scales, starting at the base of the bulb to ensure that a piece of the basal plate (the solid base of the bulb from where the roots emerge) is attached. Discard any scales that appear damaged. If you only need a few plants, remove only a few scales and then replant the bulb. However, all the scales can be snapped off if you require large numbers.

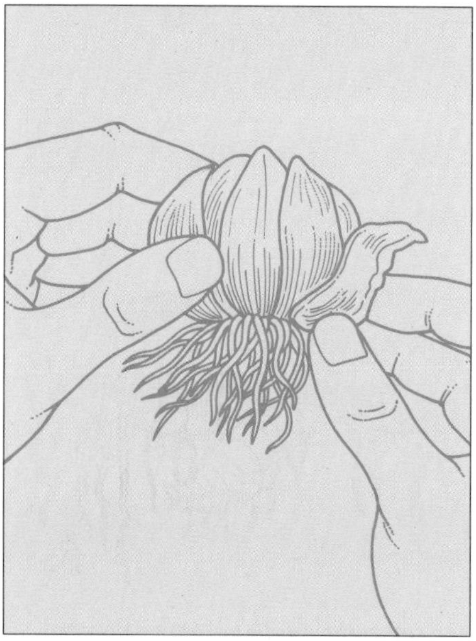

Detach whole scale leaves one by one

Place the scales in a plastic bag containing a fungicide powder, such as fine sulphur dust, and shake to coat them in the fungicide. Half-fill a plastic bag with moist vermiculite or a mixture of equal parts moist peat and perlite. Place the scales in the bag, breathe into the top to inflate it, then seal with a twist tie. Place the bag in a dark place at about 20°C (68°F).

Alternatively, fill a modular tray with equal parts moist perlite or vermiculite and multipurpose compost. Insert a scale in each module, base plate downwards, burying about half the scale. Keep the scales moist, cover and place on a heated bench or in a propagator at 20°C (68°F).

Aftercare

Check the scales for bulblet development after a few months. These tiny bulbs will appear from the basal plate. Pot them up individually without detaching the old scale leaf as it will wither away naturally as the bulblet grows. Use equal parts of soil-based compost and fine grit for potting, and top dress with further grit.

Keep in a cool shady place in summer and protect in a cold frame during winter until the bulbs are of flowering size, when they can be planted out.

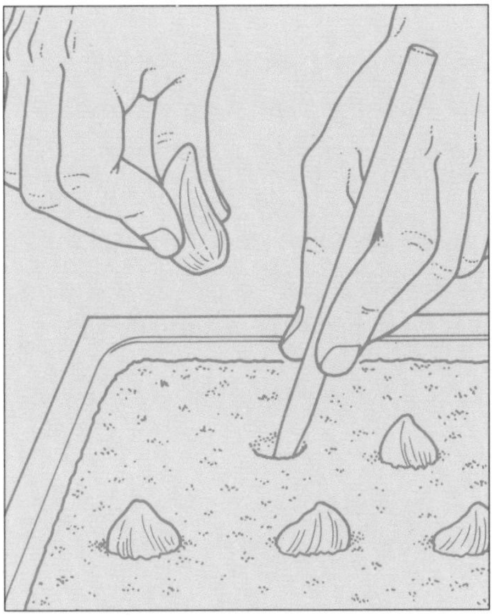

Insert vertically into moist compost

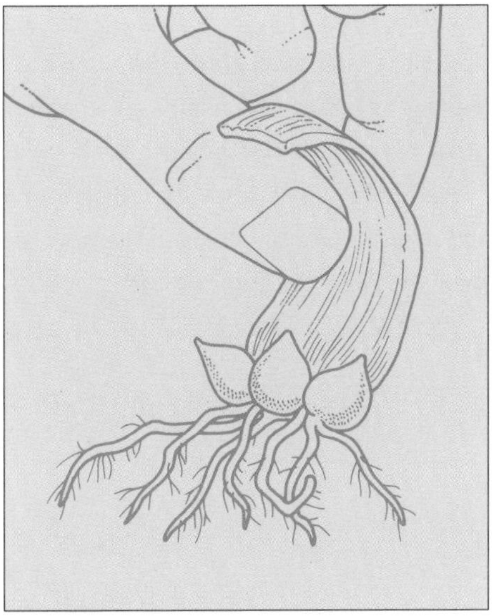

Bulbs will form at the basal plate

WHAT CAN GO WRONG

SCALES ROT AWAY

Problem: the scales have been attacked by fungal infections

Action: choose healthy scales, apply a fungicide and keep the compost just moist rather than wet

PLANTS SUITABLE FOR SCALING

Fritillaria (scaly bulbs only)	fritillary
Lilium	lily

CHIPPING

This method is used for true bulbs with tightly packed scale leaves. The bulb is cut into vertical segments like an orange, each with a section of the basal plate. The method is best carried out when food reserves in the bulb are high during dormancy. This will be in late summer or autumn for spring- and summer-flowering bulbs.

Disease can easily enter the bulb sections and cause rotting, so wash hands before you begin (or better still wear latex gloves), and ensure all tools and surfaces are clean and sterile.

Method

Lift mature bulbs when they dormant and brush off any soil. Inspect them for signs of ill health and discard any that show disease. Clean the bulbs by removing the outer layers of the papery tunic. Place the bulb on a smooth hard surface like a wall tile and use a clean, sharp knife to cut off the old roots. Leave the basal plate intact, but cut off the nose of the bulb.

Set the bulb basal plate down and cut it vertically into 8–16 sections or 'chips', making sure each one retains a piece of basal plate. Place the chips in a plastic bag containing a fungicide powder, such as fine sulphur dust, and shake to coat them.

Half-fill a plastic bag with moist vermiculite or a mixture of equal parts moist peat and perlite. Place the chips in the bag, breathe into the bag to inflate it, then seal with a twist tie. Place the bag in a dark place at about 20°C (68°F).

Alternatively, fill a modular tray with equal parts moist perlite or vermiculite and

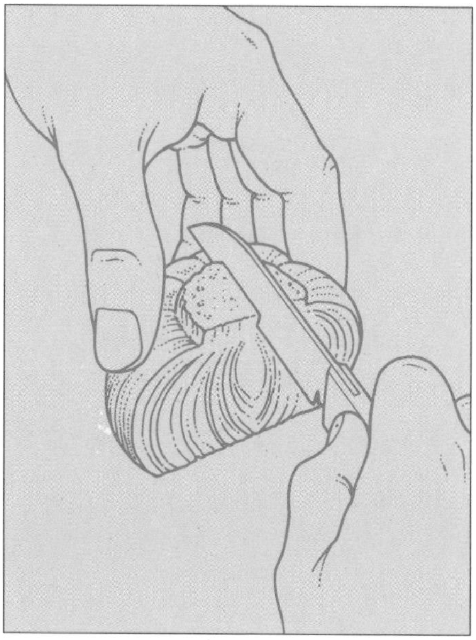

Cut the whole bulb into sections

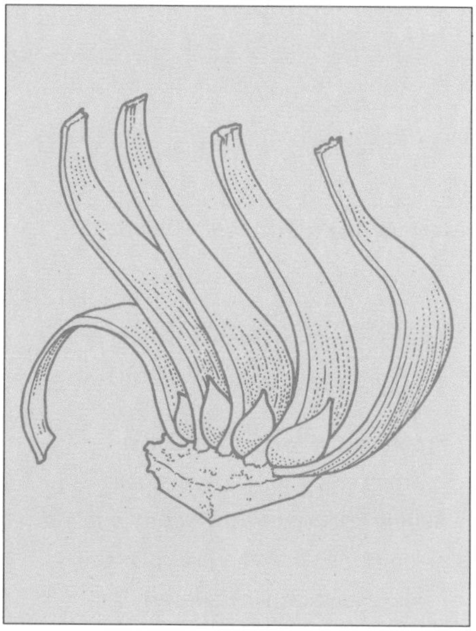

Bulblets appear between the scale leaves

multi-purpose compost. Insert a chip in each module, base plate downwards, burying about half the chip. Keep the scales moist, cover and place on a heated bench or in a propagator at 20°C (68°F).

Aftercare

Check the chips for bulblet development after a few months. The tiny bulbs will appear from the basal plate. Pot up the chips individually with the basal plate downwards. Use equal parts soil-based compost and fine grit to cover the bulblet, but leave the scale leaves exposed. These will wither away as the bulblet grows on.

Keep in a cool shady place in summer and protect in a cold frame during winter until the bulbs are of flowering size, when they can be planted out.

Snowdrops are propagated by chipping

PLANTS SUITABLE FOR CHIPPING

Allium	ornamental onion
Galanthus	snowdrop
Hippeastrum	amaryllis
Narcissus	daffodil
Nerine	jersey lily
Scilla	squill

WHAT CAN GO WRONG

CHIPS ROT AWAY

Problem: the chips have been attacked by fungal infections

Action: choose healthy bulbs, use a clean knife, apply a fungicide and keep the compost just moist rather than wet

TWIN SCALING

This method is very similar to chipping but with a minor refinement. In chipping, the bulb segments remain complete, but in twin-scaling the sections are cut again until only a pair of scale leaves are attached to the basal plate.

PLANTS SUITABLE FOR TWIN SCALING

Galanthus	snowdrop
Hyacinthus	hyacinth
Narcissus	daffodil

Method

Select, clean and trim the bulbs following the instructions described for chipping (see page 124). Once the bulb has been cut into chips, place each chip on its side and cut through the basal plate to create further sections, each with just a pair of scale leaves. This requires some patience and precision and a sharp, thin-bladed knife such as a scalpel to avoid damaging the twin scales.

Treat the twin scales with fungicide and place in a rooting medium or plant in modules as directed for chipping. Once bulblets have formed, pot them up as before.

SCORING AND SCOOPING

These methods of propagation are generally only used for hyacinths as they produce few offsets and don't come true from seed. Both involve cutting into the basal plate to increase the area for production of bulblets.

Scoring

Lift mature bulbs in mid to late summer when dormant and brush off any soil. Inspect the bulbs for signs of ill health and discard any that show disease. Clean the bulbs by

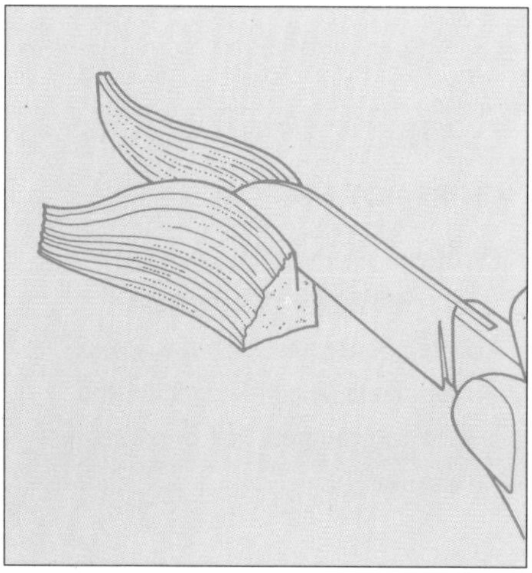

When twin scaling, trim to a pair of scales

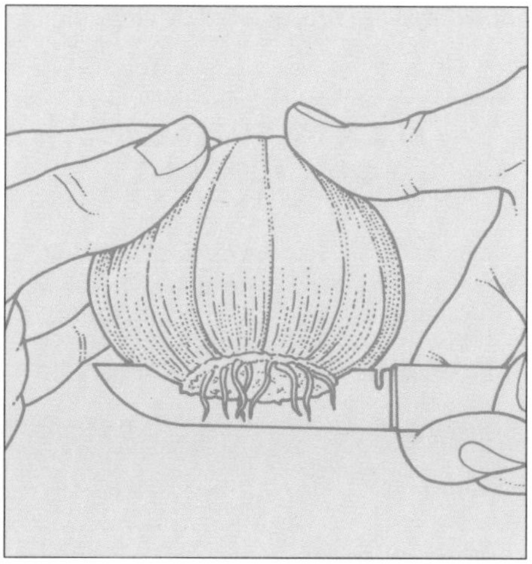

***Scoring:** trim the basal plate with a knife*

removing the outer layers of the papery tunic.

Turn the bulb upside down and use a clean, sharp knife to make two V-shaped cuts across and right through the basal plate at right angles to each other. Dust the cut surfaces with fungicide.

Place the bulb, basal plate upwards, on a seed tray filled with clean sand, perlite or vermiculite, so that the bulb is half buried. Keep moist and warm at 20–25°C (68–77°F).

Scooping

Lift, select, clean and prepare the bulb following the instructions described for scoring above. Hold the bulb upside down and very carefully scoop out the whole of the basal plate with a sharp knife or sharpened teaspoon. This can be quite tough to do if the tool isn't sharp enough. Cut deep enough to just expose the bases of the scale leaves, then dust the cut surfaces with fungicide. Continue as for scoring.

This method often produces more bulblets than scoring but they are usually of a smaller size.

Aftercare

After about ten weeks, begin to check the bulb for bulblets forming in the cut area. Transfer the bulb, bulblets uppermost, to a pot of compost so the bulblets are just covered, and place in a cold frame. Leaves should appear on the bulblets in spring.

As the leaves die back in summer, separate the bulblets and pot up individually to grow on to flowering size in three or four years.

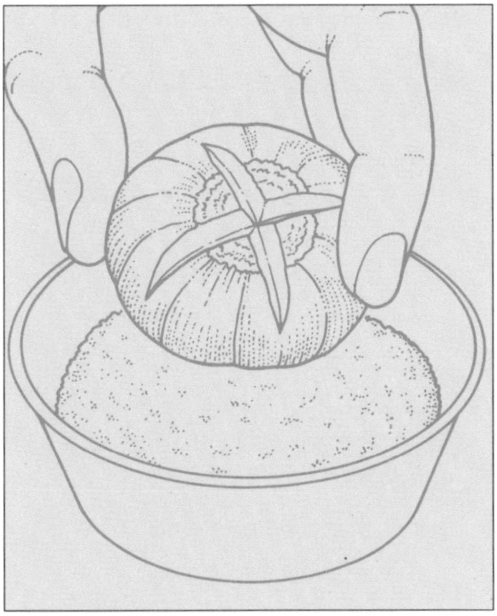

***Scoring:** half bury the bulb in sand*

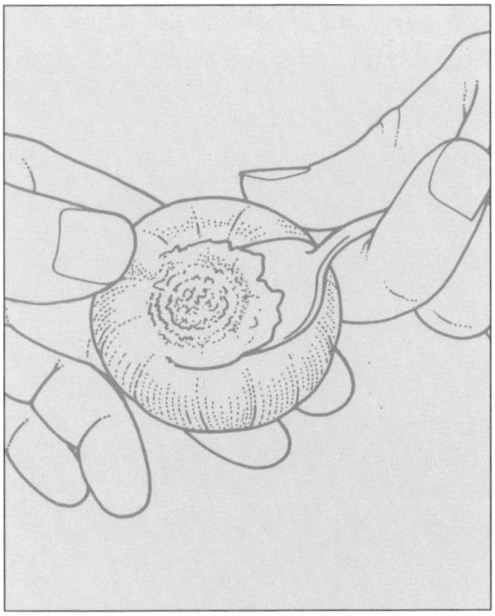

Scooping out the base of the bulb

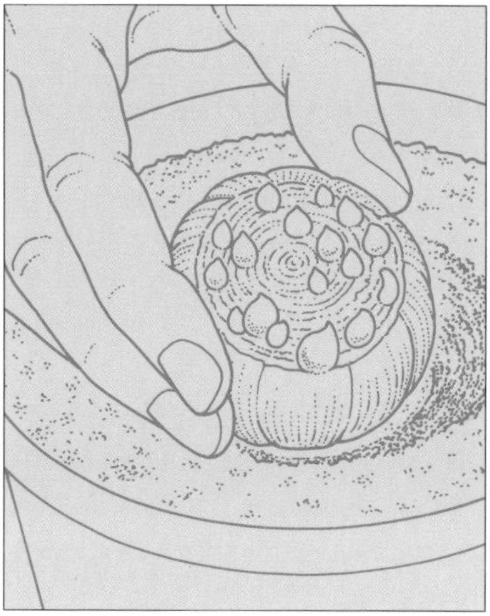

Bulblets should form on the basal plate

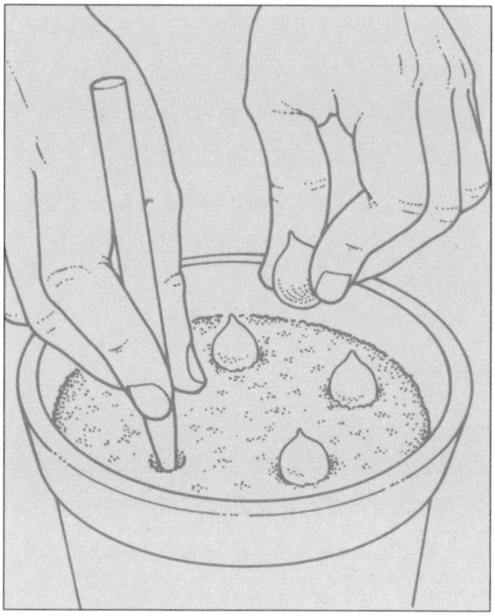

Pot up lily bulbils to root

LILY BULBILS

A few species of lilies produce small black bulbils in the leaf axils (where the leaf joins the stem). These bulbils can be removed and grown on.

Collect the bulbils at the end of the flowering period: they readily detach at this time. Lay them on a tray or pot of soil-based compost and cover with fine grit with the tips just poking through.

Place them in a cold frame and keep moist but protected until the following autumn when they can be potted up individually or planted out. They will attain flowering size in two or three years and be identical to the parent plant.

PROPAGATION EQUIPMENT

A greater success rate can be achieved with many propagation techniques if they are carried out in a warm, protected environment. A warm windowsill may be sufficient for raising a few plants, but once plants are placed away from the direct light of the window they will struggle. When space inside is limiting the opportunities for propagation, it might be time to consider acquiring other pieces of equipment to provide more space and protection from the elements.

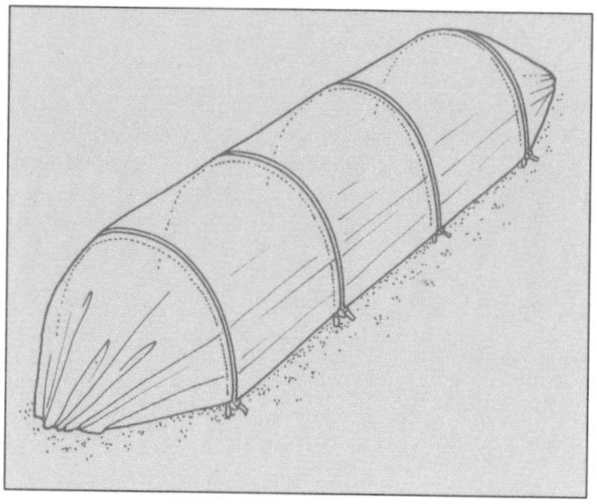

A cloche warms the soil prior to sowing

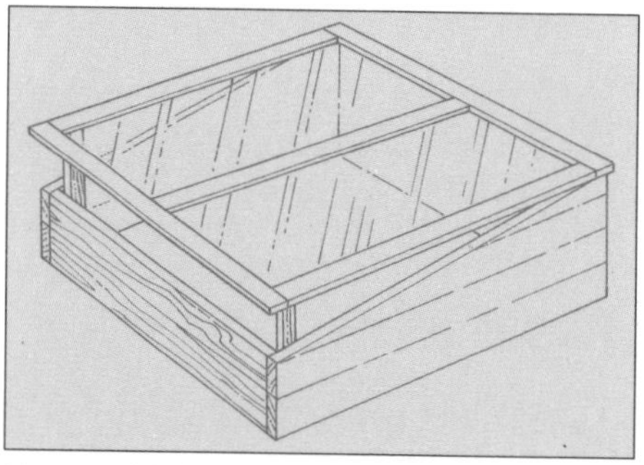

Use a cold frame for cuttings and seedlings

Cloche

This is a low tunnel which can be moved about to cover a fresh patch of soil. It will help to warm the soil in early spring or autumn to create a better environment for sowing seed outdoors and so prolong the season. Cloches are usually made of glass, polythene or fleece.

Cold frame

A cold frame has low walls and a hinged or removable lid. Most are constructed of glass and wood, polythene or polycarbonate. The base inside is often filled with a sandy soil mix so plants can be raised directly in the soil as well as in pots.

Although not heated, a cold frame offers shelter from heavy rains and wind and so creates a warmer environment. This is useful for housing easy-to-root cuttings over the winter and for preparing young plants raised in a warmer environment for tougher outdoor conditions. Seeds that need a cold period to stimulate germination can also be stored here.

Try to site the cold frame in an open position in light shade, to receive good light levels without scorching. Open the lid to ventilate on hot, sunny days but remember to close it again on cold nights.

Mini greenhouse

This can be a temporary or permanent structure, but is designed to house a series of trays or pots of plants on shelving, which is covered with glass, polycarbonate or polythene. It can be usefully set against a wall to occupy little space, but will house a good number of plants and give some protection from cold and winds.

Use a mini greenhouse to raise spring-sown seeds, store young plants and raise early or late summer cuttings. A permanent lean-to mini greenhouse could also accommodate slow-growing hardy plant seedlings or late-rooted cuttings ready for potting in spring.

Place in a well-lit position and be prepared to ventilate well by opening the door on warm days in spring and summer. Young plants will dry out quickly, so maintain humidity by watering regularly early and late in the day, or by setting a tray of gravel in water in the base.

Free-standing greenhouse

A full-size greenhouse offers plenty of space for propagation as well as growing mature plants. It should be sited away from the shade of trees in an open position to maximise light levels in the winter months. Choose a sheltered position away from the cooling effect of strong winds.

An unheated greenhouse will suffer low night time temperatures from late autumn to early spring, which may rule out some propagation techniques. Using a maximum/minimum thermometer will help to monitor conditions so you can decide what is possible.

To reduce heat loss in the colder months, insulate all or part of the greenhouse by attaching bubble wrap to the walls. In the summer, shading may need to be applied to prevent tender young plants scorching in the stronger sun. Apply a shading paint or fix shade netting to the walls.

GREENHOUSE HEATING

Heating will raise the ambient temperature in a greenhouse both during the day and at night.

- **Paraffin or propane heater** These help increase the temperature, but also produce condensation which can cause fungal spoilage at low temperatures when ventilation is poor.
- **Electric tubular heater** This uses low energy to maintain the temperature just above freezing with thermostatic controls.
- **Electric fan heater** Using a greater amount of electricity, this heats the air and blows it around to provide an even temperature with air movement to prevent fungal rot. The temperature can be maintained with thermostatic controls.
- **Heated cables** These can be installed on greenhouse benching, either as part of a heated mat or set into a sand bench. They usually come with thermostatic controls and deliver heat to the base of seed trays and pots, encouraging fast rooting of cuttings and speeding up seed germination. If the bench is covered with polythene or bubble wrap, the warm air and moisture from the compost is trapped within the 'tent' so creating a warm, humid atmosphere that is ideal for cuttings and young seedlings. The seedlings and rooted cuttings can then be moved to the open benches of a warm greenhouse to acclimatize.

PLANT
DIRECTORY

Sunflower (Helianthus annus)

ANNUALS, BIENNIALS AND BEDDING

Hardy annuals

The seeds from this group of plants can be sown direct into the soil, or into containers under cover and then planted out as young plants. If sown direct they should be thinned out in stages (see page 22), by removing crowded seedlings to a final spacing of 15–30 cm (6–12 in). Young transplants should be given the same spacing. This allows the plants to grow into healthy, sturdy plants which will flower for longer than their overcrowded counterparts.

Some hardy annuals can also be sown in autumn and allowed to overwinter as small plants. Although they will come into flower earlier, there may be greater losses.

BOTANICAL NAME	COMMON NAME	SOWING TIME	SOWING TEMPERATURE	GERMINATION PERIOD	NOTES
Agrostemma	**corn cockle**	March, Sept	20–25°C (68–77°F)	7–14 days	good cut flower
Ammi majus	**Queen Anne's lace**	March, Sept	15–17°C (59–63°F)	7–21 days	good cut flower
Calendula	**pot marigold**	March–April	17–25°C (63–77°F)	7–21 days	self seeds
Centaurea	**cornflower**	March	15–25°C (59–77°F)	10–14 days	good cut flower
Cerinthe major	**honeywort**	March, Sept	17–25°C (63–77°F)	5–21 days	attractive to bees
Chrysanthemum		March	15–25°C (59–77°F)	10–15 days	
Consolida	**larkspur**	March, Sept	13–16°C (55–61°F)	30 days	
Eschscholzia	**Californian poppy**	March, Sept	15–20°C (59–68°F)	10–12 days	self seeds
Euphorbia oblongata		March	17–21°C (63–70°F)	15–21 days	good cut flower
Godetia		March, Sept	15–25°C (59–77°F)	10–14 days	
Helianthus	**sunflower**	March	20–25°C (68–77°F)	21 days	good cut flower
Iberis	**candytuft**	March, Sept	15–25°C (59–77°F)	21 days	
Lathyrus odoratus	**sweet pea**	March, Sept	15–25°C (59–77°F)	7–21 days	good cut flower
Lavatera	**mallow**	March	15–25°C (59–77°F)	14–30 days	
Lobularia	**candytuft**	March, Sept	15–25°C (59–77°F)	21 days	
Limnanthes	**poached egg flower**	March, Sept	10–15°C (50–59°F)	14–21 days	self seeds
Linum grandiflorum	**flax**	March	17–25°C (63–77°F)	14–21 days	
Nemophila	**baby blue eyes**	March, Sept	5–15°C (41–59°F)	14–30 days	self seeds
Nicandra	**shoo fly plant**	March	17–25°C (63–77°F)	7–21 days	poisonous if eaten
Nigella	**love-in-a-mist**	March, Sept	17–25°C (63–77°F)	14–30 days	self seeds
Papaver	**opium poppy**	March, Sept	10–20°C (50–68°F)	14–21 days	self seeds
Phacelia	**Californian bluebell**	March, Sept	17–25°C (63–77°F)	14–21 days	attractive to bees
Salvia horminium	**clary sage**	March, Sept	15–25°C (59–77°F)	7–21 days	good cut flower
Tropaeolum majus	**nasturtium**	March	20–25°C (68–77°F)	7–12 days	edible flowers

Biennials

True biennials grow from seed and need a chill before they flower in the second season, set seed and die. However, there are also plants that are perennial in habit, but their flowering performance is initially striking before it tails off as the plants mature. These are often treated as biennials and discarded after one flowering season even though they may not actually die. Many spring bedding plants are used in this way.

BOTANICAL NAME	COMMON NAME	SOWING TIME	GERMINATION PERIOD	FLOWERING TIME (FOLLOWING YEAR)	NOTES
Bellis perennis	**double daisy**	May–June	7–21 days	March–July	spring bedding
Campanula medium	**Canterbury bell**	April–May	10–12 days	May–July	
Dianthus barbatus	**sweet William**	May–June	14–21 days	June –July	good cut flower
Digitalis purpurea	**foxglove**	June–July	14–30 days	May–July	
Dipsacus fullonum	**teasel**	June–July	20–120 days	July–Aug	self seeds
Eryngium giganteum	**sea holly**	June–July	60–100 days	June–Aug	self seeds
Erysimum chieri	**wallflower**	May–June	7–14 days	April –June	
Hesperis matronalis	**sweet rocket**	April–May	15–60 days	May–June	fragrant
Lunaria annua	**honesty**	June–July	14–21 days	April–June	
Matthiola incana	**Brompton stock**	June–July	7–21 days	May–June	over-winter under glass
Myosotis	**forget-me-not**	May–July	14–30 days	April–June	spring bedding
Oenothera biennis	**evening primrose**	June–July	14–30 days	June–Oct	self seeds
Papaver croceum	**Iceland poppy**	May–June	14–30 days	June–Aug	
Primula hybrids	**Polyanthus**	May–July	10–30 days	Jan–June	spring bedding
Verbascum bombyciferum	**mullein**	April	14–30 days	June–Aug	self seeds
Viola x wittrockiana	**winter pansy**	May–June	14–21 days	Oct–April	winter/spring bedding

Summer bedding and patio plants

These plants are mostly half-hardy annuals or tender perennials. Many can be grown from seed, but they will need higher temperatures than those required by hardy plants. They are often slower to mature and flower than hardy annuals so some need to be sown earlier in the year if they are to reach flowering size by June, when in most areas the danger of a late frost has definitely passed.

BOTANICAL NAME	COMMON NAME	SOWING TIME	SOWING TEMP	GERMINATION PERIOD	NOTES
Ageratum	**ageratum**	Feb–April	20–25°C (68–77°F)	7–21 days	needs light to germinate
Antirrhinum	**snapdragon**	Feb–March	17–25°C (63–77°F)	10–21 days	germinates better in light
Begonia	**fibrous begonia**	Dec–March	18–25°C (64–77°F)	15–40 days	needs light to germinate
Bidens		March	17–25°C (63–77°F)	10–21 days	
Cleome	**spider flower**	March	18–25°C (64–77°F)	10–21 days	
Cosmos	**cosmea**	March–May	18–25°C (64–77°F)	7–14 days	can be sown direct in May
Dahlia	**bedding dahlia**	Feb–April	17–25°C (63–77°F)	7–21 days	
Diascia	**twinspur**	March–April	21–25°C (70–77°F)	14–21 days	
Eustoma	**lisianthus**	Feb–April	21–25°C (70–77°F)	14–30 days	long-lasting cut flower
Gazania	**treasure flower**	Feb	17–25°C (63–77°F)	14–30 days	
Impatiens	**busy lizzie**	March–April	20–25°C (68–77°F)	10–21 days	needs light to germinate
Ipomoea	**morning glory**	March–April	20–25°C (68–77°F)	7–30 days	scarify seed before sowing
Isotoma	**laurentia**	Dec–Jan	17–20°C (63–68°F)	10–28 days	
Lobelia		Jan–March	17–25°C (63–77°F)	14–21 days	needs light to germinate
Mimulus	**monkey flower**	Feb–April	17–25°C (63–77°F)	7–21 days	germinates better in light
Moluccella	**bells of Ireland**	March–April	17–25°C (63–77°F)	14–21 days	pre-chill for two weeks
Nemesia		March–April	15–20°C (59–68°F)	7–21 days	germinates better in the dark
Nicotiana	**tobacco plant**	Feb–April	17–25°C (63–77°F)	7–21 days	needs light to germinate
Pelargonium	**geranium**	Jan–Feb	21–24°C (70–75°F)	3–21 days	
Petunia		March–April	20–25°C (68–77°F)	10–21 days	germinates better in light
Phlox drummondii		March–April	22–25°C (72–77°F)	10–21 days	germinates best in the dark
Rhodochiton	**purple bell vine**	Feb–March	15–25°C (59–77°F)	12–40 days	
Ricinus	**castor oil plant**	March–April	17–25°C (63–77°F)	15–20 days	seeds poisonous if eaten
Rudbeckia	**cone flower**	March–April	17–25°C (63–77°F)	7–21 days	
Salpiglossis	**painted tongue**	March–April	17–25°C (63–77°F)	14–30 days	
Salvia	**painted sage**	March–April	17–25°C (63–77°F)	7–21 days	germinates better in light
Senecio		Jan–Feb	15–25°C (59–77°F)	10–21 days	silver foliage plant
Tagetes erecta	**African marigold**	Feb	18–25°C (64–77°F)	4–21 days	sow seed flat
Tagetes patula	**French marigold**	April	18–25°C (64–77°F)	4–21 days	sow seed flat
Verbena	**vervain**	Feb–March	18–25°C (64–77°F)	7–28 days	germinates best in the dark
Viola	**viola, pansy**	March–April	10–22°C (50–72°F)	14–21 days	germinates best in the dark
Zinnia		March–April	17–25°C (63–77°F)	10–24 days	

PERENNIALS

A range of popular hardy and tender perennials are listed here. If in doubt as to how to propagate a favourite perennial, look at its growth habit to determine whether it can be divided or whether there is suitable stem growth for cutting material then follow the instructions for a listed plant with a similar habit.

BOTANICAL NAME	COMMON NAME	METHOD	DIFFICULTY	WHEN	NOTES
Acanthus HARDY	**bear's breeches**	division	+	spring or autumn	
		seed	++	spring	sow at 15°C (59°F)
		root cuttings	+	autumn	
Achillea HARDY	**yarrow**	division	+	spring	
		seed	+	spring or autumn	sow at 15°C (59°F)
		basal cuttings	+	spring	
		semi-ripe cuttings	+	summer	
Alchemilla mollis HARDY	**lady's mantle**	division	+	spring	
		seed	+	spring or autumn	sow at 15°C (59°F)
Anthemis tinctoria HARDY	**golden marguerite**	seed	+	spring	sow at 15°C (59°F)
		basal cuttings	+	spring	
		semi-ripe cuttings	+	summer	
Aquilegia HARDY	**columbine**	division	+	spring or autumn	
		seed	+	spring to summer	sow fresh seed
				autumn	sow old seed
Argyranthemum TENDER	**marguerite**	stem tip cuttings	+	spring or summer	
Aster HARDY	**michaelmas daisy**	division	+	spring or autumn	
		seed	+	spring	sow at 15°C (59°F)
		basal cuttings	+	spring	
Astilbe HARDY	**goatsbeard**	division	++	early spring	
		seed	++	autumn	chill before sowing
Bergenia HARDY	**elephant's ears**	division	+	spring or autumn	
		seed	++	spring	
Brunnera HARDY		division	+	after flowering	
		seed	+	spring	sow at 10°C (50°F)
		root cuttings	+	winter	
Campanula HARDY	**bell flower**	division	+	spring or autumn	
		seed	+	spring	
		basal cuttings	++	spring	
Canna TENDER	**canna lily**	division	+	spring	
		seed	+++	spring	scarify, then sow at 21°C (70°F)
Carex HARDY	**sedge**	division	+	spring	
		seeds	++	spring	seeds are short lived
Chrysanthemum HARDY		division	+	spring	
		seeds	+	spring	
		basal cuttings	+	spring	

KEY: + = easy, ++ = needs care, +++ = expect failures

Dahlia TENDER		division seed basal cuttings	+ + +	spring spring spring	 sow at 17–21°C (63–70°F)
Delphinium HARDY		division seed basal stem cuttings	+ + +	spring spring spring	 sow at 13°C (55°F)
Dianthus HARDY	**pink, carnation**	division seed pipings layering	++ + + ++	summer or autumn spring summer mid to late summer	 for pinks for carnations
Diascia HARDY/TENDER		stem tip cuttings	+	spring or late summer	
Dicentra HARDY	**bleeding heart**	division root cuttings	++ +	spring winter	easy to damage roots
Doronicum HARDY	**leopard's bane**	division seed	+ +	after flowering early spring	 sow at 10°C (50°F)
Echinacea HARDY	**purple coneflower**	division seed root cuttings	+ + ++	spring spring autumn	 sow at 10°C (50°F)
Echinops HARDY	**globe thistle**	division seed root cuttings	++ + +	spring spring late autumn	 sow at 15°C (59°F)
Epimedium HARDY	**barrenwort**	division	+	spring	
Euphorbia HARDY	**spurge**	division seed basal cuttings semi-ripe cuttings	+ + ++ ++	spring spring or autumn spring summer	 sow at 15°C (59°F) sap is an irritant
Festuca glauca HARDY	**sheep's fescue**	division seed	+ +	spring or autumn spring or autumn	 sow at 15°C (59°F)
Filipendula HARDY	**meadow sweet**	division seed	+ ++	spring spring	 sow at 10°C (50°F)
Gaura HARDY	**whirling butterfly**	division seed basal cuttings semi-ripe cuttings	++ + ++ ++	spring spring spring summer	 sow at 10°C (50°F)
Geranium HARDY	**cranesbill**	division seed basal stem cuttings root cuttings	+ + ++ +	spring or late summer early summer late spring autumn	 sow at 15°C (59°F) few varieties
Geum HARDY	**avens**	division seed	+ ++	spring spring or autumn	 sow at 10°C (50°F)
Helleborus HARDY	**hellebore**	division seed	+ +	after flowering summer	 sow fresh
Helichrysum petiolare TENDER		softwood cuttings semi-ripe cuttings	+ +	spring summer	
Hemerocallis HARDY	**day lily**	division seed	+ +	spring to autumn spring or autumn	 sow at 15°C (59°F)

Heuchera	**coral bells**	division	+	spring or autumn	
HARDY		seed	+	spring	sow at 10°C (50°F)
		stem tip cuttings	++	spring or summer	
Hosta	**plantain lily**	division	+	early spring	
HARDY		seed	++	spring	sow at 15°C (59°F)
Iris, rhizomatous		division	+	after flowering	
HARDY		seed	++	autumn	soak seed for 48 hours
Knautia H		division	+	spring	
HARDY		seed	+	spring	sow at 15°C (59°F)
		basal stem cuttings	++	spring	
Kniphofia	**red hot poker**	division	++	late spring	
HARDY		seed	+	spring	sow at 15°C (59°F)
Liatris	**blazing star**	division	+	spring	
HARDY		seed	++	spring	sow at 15°C (59°F)
Liriope	**lily turf**	division	+	spring	
HARDY		seed	+	October	extract seed from berries
Lupinus	**lupin**	seed	+	early spring	sow at 15°C (59°F)
HARDY		basal stem cuttings	++	spring	
Malva	**mallow**	seed	+	spring	sow at 10°C (50°F)
HARDY		basal cuttings	+	spring	
Miscanthus		division	+	early summer	
HARDY					
Musa	**banana**	division	+++	spring	remove offsets (tender)
		seed	++	spring	scarify and soak in hot water
Ophiopogon planiscapus nigrescens		division	+	spring	
HARDY		seed	+	October	extract seed from berries
Osteospermum		seed	+	spring	sow at 18°C (64°F)
TENDER		softwood cuttings	+	spring	
		semi-ripe cuttings	+	summer	
Paeonia	**peony**	division	+	early spring / autumn	
HARDY		seed	++	autumn	seeds require a double chill
Papaver orientale	**oriental poppy**	division	+	spring	
HARDY		seed	+	summer	need light to germinate
		root cuttings	+	winter	
Pelargonium	**geranium**	seeds	+	mid spring	
TENDER		softwood cuttings	+	spring or summer	root at 18°C (64°F)
		semi-ripe cuttings	+	late summer	root at 15°C (59°F)
Penstemon		seed	+	spring	
TENDER/HARDY		semi-ripe cuttings	+	summer	
Phlox paniculata		division	+	spring or autumn	
HARDY		seed	+	early spring	sow at 15°C (59°F)
		stem tip cuttings	+	spring	alpine forms
		root cuttings	+	winter	border forms
Polygonatum	**solomon's seal**	division	+	autumn to early spring	
HARDY					
Primula	**primrose**	division	++	after flowering	
HARDY		seed	+	late summer	sow fresh at 15°C (59°F)
		root cuttings	++	winter	good for P. denticulata

Pulmonaria HARDY	**lungwort**	division seed root cuttings	+ + +	after flowering spring winter	 sow at 10°C (50°F)
Rheum HARDY	**ornamental rhubarb**	division seed	+ +	late winter autumn	 sow at 10°C (50°F)
Rodgersia HARDY		division seed	+ +	spring or autumn spring	 sow at 10°C (50°F)
Rudbeckia HARDY	**coneflower**	division seed	+ +	spring or autumn spring or summer	 sow at 10°C (50°F)
Salvia HARDY/TENDER	**sage**	division seed basal stem cuttings stem tip cuttings semi-ripe cuttings	+ + + + +	spring spring late spring spring summer	border forms sow at 16–18°C (61–64°F) tender forms tender and hardy forms
Saxifraga HARDY	**saxifrage**	division	+	after flowering	remove offsets
Schizostylis HARDY	**kaffir lily**	division	+	spring	
Sedum HARDY	**iceplant**	division seed stem tip cuttings	+ + +	spring spring spring or summer	 sow at 13°C (55°F)
Sidalcea HARDY	**prairie mallow**	division seed basal stem cuttings	+ + +	spring or autumn spring spring	 sow at 10°C (50°F)
Solenostemon TENDER	**coleus**	seed softwood cuttings	+ +	spring spring or summer	sow at 18°C (64°F)
Stipa gigantea HARDY	**feather grass**	division seed	++ +	spring spring	don't divide too small sow at 15°C (59°F)
Thalictrum HARDY	**meadow rue**	division seed	+ ++	spring spring	plants slow to establish sow fresh seed
Tiarella HARDY	**foam flower**	division seed	++ +	spring or autumn autumn	 need a winter chill
Trillium HARDY	**wake robin**	division seed scoring	+ +++ ++	after flowering autumn after flowering	 need a winter chill score the rhizome
Verbascum HARDY	**mullein**	division seed root cuttings	+ + +	spring spring late autumn	 sow at 15°C (59°F)
Verbena HARDY	**vervain**	division seed softwood cuttings	+ + +	spring spring late spring	border forms sow at 15°C (59°F)
Viola HARDY	**violet**	division seed softwood cuttings mounding	+ + + +	spring or autumn spring spring summer	 sow at 15°C (59°F)
Zantedeschia HARDY	**arum lily**	division seed	+ ++	spring spring	 sow at 21°C (70°F)

SHRUBS

Knowing how to propagate a range of shrubs can come in handy. Not all shrubs live long so it is advisable to raise some replacements before the parent fades and dies. You may also need a large number of plants to grow an informal or formal hedge. The list of shrubs available to gardeners is endless, so only key plants are listed here.

Summer flowers of fuchsia

BOTANICAL NAME	COMMON NAME	METHOD	DIFFICULTY	WHEN	NOTES
Abelia		softwood cuttings	+	spring	
		hardwood cuttings	++	September	root in a cold frame
Aucuba	**spotted laurel**	semi-ripe cuttings	+	summer	reduce foliage
		simple layering	+	spring or autumn	
		seed	+	autumn	sow fresh seed
Berberis	**barberry**	semi-ripe cuttings	+	summer	heel or basal
		hardwood cuttings	++	winter	
		seed	+	winter	chill before sowing
Buddleja	**butterfly bush**	semi-ripe cuttings	+	summer	
		hardwood cuttings	+	winter	
		seed	+	spring	sow direct at 10°C (50°F)
Buxus	**box**	semi-ripe cuttings	+	late summer	heel or basal
		division	+	spring	remove suckers
		seed	++	winter	chill before sowing
Camellia		semi-ripe cuttings	++	summer	stem tip or leaf bud
		hardwood cuttings	+++	autumn/winter	bottom heat 12–20°C (52–68°F)
		simple layering	+	spring	slow to root

KEY: + = easy, ++ = needs care, +++ = expect failures

Calluna	**heather**	semi-ripe cuttings	+	summer	remove flower buds
		simple layering	+	spring	
		mound layering	+	spring	
Ceanothus	**Californian lilac**	softwood cuttings	+	late spring	deciduous types
		semi-ripe cuttings	++	summer	evergreen types
Choisya	**Mexican orange**	semi-ripe cuttings	+	summer	
		hardwood cuttings	+	winter	root in frost-free site
Cistus	**sun rose**	softwood cuttings	++	late spring or summer	
		semi-ripe cuttings	+	mid summer or autumn	
		seed	+	spring	
Cornus	**dogwood**	hardwood cuttings	+	winter	
		seed	+	autumn	chill before sowing
		division	+	early spring	for *C. stolonifera*
Cotinus	**smoke bush**	softwood cuttings	+++	spring	
		seed	++	late summer	sow fresh seed
		simple layering	+	winter	
		French layering	+	spring	
Cotoneaster		softwood cuttings	+	spring or summer	
		hardwood cuttings	++	autumn	
		seed	++	spring	need hot and cold prior to sowing
Daphne		semi-ripe cuttings	++	summer	
		root cuttings	+	autumn or winter	
		simple or air layering	+	late spring	
		grafting	+++	winter	side veneer, whip and tongue, or apical wedge
Deutzia		semi-ripe cuttings	+	summer	
		hardwood cuttings	++	winter	root under cover
Elaeagnus		semi-ripe cuttings	++	summer	bottom heat 15–20°C (59–68°F)
		hardwood cuttings	++	winter	bottom heat 20°C (68°F)
		seed	+	autumn	chill before sowing
Erica	**heath**	semi-ripe cuttings	+	summer	remove flower buds
		simple layering	+	spring	
		mound layering	+	spring	
Escallonia		semi-ripe cuttings	+	summer	
		hardwood cuttings	+	winter	root in frost-free site
Euonymus	**spindle**	softwood cuttings	+	spring	
		semi-ripe cuttings	+	summer	
		seed	++	autumn	remove outer flesh seeds are poisonous
Fatsia	**castor oil plant**	semi-ripe cuttings	++	summer	shoot tip, keep two leaves only
		seed	+	autumn or spring	sow at 15–20°C (59–68°F)
Forsythia		softwood cuttings	+	spring	
		hardwood cuttings	+	winter	
		simple layering	+	spring	
Fuchsia		softwood cuttings	+	spring or summer	rarely fail to root
		semi-ripe cuttings	+	spring or summer	rarely fail to root
		hardwood cuttings	+	winter	*F. magellanica*

Hebe	**veronica**	softwood cuttings	+	spring/summer	
		semi-ripe cuttings	+	summer	small-leaved types
Hydrangea		softwood cuttings	+	late spring or summer	reduce leaves by half
		semi-ripe cuttings	+	midsummer	
		hardwood cuttings	+	winter	
Hypericum	**rose of Sharon**	semi-ripe cuttings	+	midsummer	
		hardwood cuttings	+	winter	root in deep pots
		division	+	spring	*H. calycinum*
Kerria	**jew's mantle**	hardwood cuttings	+	winter	
		division	+	spring	
Kolkwitzia	**beauty bush**	softwood cuttings	+	spring	
		semi-ripe cuttings	+	late summer	
Lavandula	**lavender**	softwood cuttings	+	spring	
		semi-ripe cuttings	++	summer	heel
		seed	++	spring	chill for four weeks
		mound layering	+	spring	
Lavatera	**mallow**	softwood cuttings	+	spring	internodal
Ligustrum	**privet**	semi-ripe cuttings	+	summer	
		hardwood cuttings	+	autumn or midwinter	root in open ground
		simple layering	+	spring	
Lonicera	**shrubby honeysuckle**	semi-ripe cuttings	+	summer	
		hardwood cuttings	+	late autumn	
		simple layering	++	spring	
Magnolia		softwood cuttings	++	late spring	wound stem
		simple layering	++	spring	
		grafting	+++	autumn	side-veneer, chip bud
Mahonia		semi-ripe cuttings	++	summer	leaf bud, root at 20°C (68°F)
		hardwood cuttings	+	winter	
		division	+	spring	
Olearia	**daisy bush**	semi-ripe cuttings	++	summer	
		hardwood cuttings	+	winter	
Osmanthus		semi-ripe cuttings	++	late summer	heel, root at 15°C (59°F)
		simple layering	++	autumn	
Perovskia	**Russian sage**	softwood cuttings	++	spring	remove flower buds
		hardwood cuttings	+	winter	root in frost-free site
Philadelphus	**mock orange**	softwood cuttings	+	spring	
		semi-ripe cuttings	+	summer	
		hardwood cuttings	+	winter	root in open ground
		seed	++	spring	fresh seed, chill before sowing
Phlomis	**Jerusalem sage**	semi-ripe cuttings	++	summer	
		seed	+	spring	
Phormium	**New Zealand flax**	division	+	spring	cut fleshy roots
		seed	++	spring	sow at 18°C (64°F)
Photinia		semi-ripe cuttings	++	summer	nodal
		seed	++	spring	

Rhododendron		softwood cuttings	++	late spring	for azaleas
		semi-ripe cuttings	++	summer	root at 12–20°C (52–68°F)
		simple layering	+	spring	
		air layering	++	spring	
		grafting	+++	winter	side-veneer
Rosa	**rose**	softwood cuttings	++	spring	
		hardwood cuttings	+	autumn	root in open ground
		division	+	spring	*R. rugosa*
		grafting	+++	summer	T-budding
Salix	**willow**	hardwood cuttings	+	autumn or winter	
		seed	+++	spring	keep moist, sow fresh seed
Sambucus	**elder**	semi-ripe cuttings	++	summer	stems can rot
		hardwood cuttings	+	winter	heel
		seed	++	autumn	chill before sowing
Santolina	**cotton lavender**	semi-ripe cuttings	+	late summer	
Spiraea		softwood cuttings	+	spring	
		semi-ripe cuttings	+	summer	
		hardwood cuttings	++	winter	
Symphoricarpos	**snowberry**	semi-ripe cuttings	+	summer	remove flower buds
		hardwood cuttings	+	winter	
		division	++	autumn to spring	cut rooted suckers
Syringa	**lilac**	root cuttings	+	autumn	
		simple layering	+	spring	
		grafting	+++	winter	apical wedge
Tamarix	**tamarisk**	hardwood cuttings	+	autumn	root in frost-free site
		seed	+	spring	
Viburnum		softwood cuttings	++	spring	deciduous types
		semi-ripe cuttings	+	summer	evergreen types
		hardwood cuttings	+	winter	root at 12–20°C (52–68°F)
		seed	+++	autumn	need hot and cold prior to sowing
Vinca	**periwinkle**	semi-ripe cuttings	+	summer or autumn	
		division	+	spring	
Weigela		semi-ripe cuttings	+	summer	
		hardwood cuttings	+	winter	root in open ground
		seed	++	spring	
Yucca		root cuttings	++	spring	remove swollen bud
		division	+	spring	remove offsets
		seed	+	spring	sow at 15°C (59°F)

CLIMBERS

Climbers are plants that grow upwards, using their ability to attach to support structures or other plants. They include plants with a variety of different life cycles – some are annuals, others perennial – and different growth habits. Of the perennial climbers, only one or two are herbaceous; most have woody stems from which they send out new soft growth every year. The method best suited to propagating climbers depends on how they grow. Annual climbers are grown from seed, while a selection of the most popular perennial climbers are included here.

Honeysuckle (Lonicera periclymenum)

BOTANICAL NAME	COMMON NAME	METHOD	DIFFICULTY	WHEN	NOTES
Actinidia HARDY	**Chinese gooseberry**	semi-ripe cuttings hardwood cuttings simple layering	++ + +	summer winter autumn	
Bougainvillea TENDER		semi-ripe cuttings hardwood cuttings layering	++ ++ +	summer winter spring	heel cuttings root at 21°C (70°F) layer into pots
Clematis HARDY	**old man's beard**	softwood cuttings semi-ripe cuttings layering grafting	+ + + +++	spring summer spring winter	leaf bud cuttings leaf bud cuttings apical wedge graft, use *C. vitalba* rootstock
Campsis HARDY	**trumpet vine**	semi-ripe cuttings hardwood cuttings root cuttings simple layering	++ + ++ +	summer winter winter autumn	
Eccremocarpus HARDY	**Chilean glory vine**	seed	+	spring	sow at 15°C (59°F)
Hedera HARDY	**ivy**	semi-ripe cuttings hardwood cuttings layering	+ ++ +	summer autumn any time	leaf bud cuttings simple or serpentine
Humulus HARDY	**hop**	semi-ripe cuttings layering root cuttings	++ + ++	summer spring winter	leaf bud serpentine
Jasminum HARDY/TENDER	**jasmine**	semi-ripe cuttings hardwood cuttings simple layering	++ + ++	summer winter spring	 hardy forms
Lonicera HARDY	**honeysuckle**	semi-ripe cuttings hardwood layering	++ + ++	summer winter spring	leaf bud serpentine
Parthenocissus HARDY	**Virginia creeper**	semi-ripe cuttings hardwood cuttings layering	+ + ++	summer winter summer	 serpentine
Passiflora HARDY/TENDER	**passion flower**	semi-ripe cuttings seed layering	+ + +	summer summer spring	 soak in hot water serpentine
Plumbago TENDER	**Cape figwort**	semi-ripe cuttings seed	+ +	summer spring	 sow at 15°C (59°F)
Solanum HARDY	**potato vine**	semi-ripe cuttings seed	+++ ++	summer spring	use side shoots sow at 20°C (68°F)
Trachelospermum HARDY	**star jasmine**	semi-ripe cuttings layering	+++ +	summer spring	root at 21°C (70°F) serpentine
Vitis HARDY	**grape vine**	semi-ripe cuttings hardwood cuttings layering	+ + +	summer winter spring	
Wisteria HARDY		softwood cuttings hardwood cuttings layering grafting	+ + + +++	late spring winter spring late winter	use side shoots serpentine apical wedge graft

HERBS

A plant is classed as a herb if any part of it can be used for food, flavouring, scent or medicine. Many plants that we grow in the garden may have been used in these ways in past times, making the list of plants that can be classed as herbs surprisingly long, so only a few culinary herbs are included here. As they are classed by their use, this group includes plants of different growth habits with different methods of propagation.

Bay (*Laurus nobilis*) EVERGREEN TREE

- Simple layering in spring.
- Semi-ripe heel cuttings of side shoots in late summer.

Basil (*Ocinum basilicum*) Half-hardy annual

- Sow seed under cover at 18–21°C (64–70°F) in late spring. Harden off thoroughly before growing outside in June.

Borage (*Borago officinalis*) HARDY ANNUAL

- Sow seed direct into prepared soil in spring or autumn. Self seeds readily.

Chives (*Allium schoenoprasum*) HARDY PERENNIAL

- Sow seed at 18°C (64°F) in spring.
- Divide clumps down to 6–10 bulbs in spring or autumn.

Coriander (*Coriandrum sativum*) HARDY ANNUAL

- Sow seeds direct into prepared soil in spring. Thin seedlings to 5 cm (2 in) apart if you intend to harvest the leaves, 23 cm (9 in) apart for seeds.

Fennel (*Foeniculum vulgare*) HARDY PERENNIAL

- Sow seed under cover at 18°C (64°F) in early spring, or sow direct into prepared soil in late spring.
- Divide clumps in autumn.

Ginger (*Zingiber officinale*) TENDER PERENNIAL

- Divide the tuberous rhizome as it starts to sprout in spring.

Lemon balm (*Melissa officinalis*) HARDY PERENNIAL

- Divide clumps in spring or autumn.
- Softwood cuttings of new shoots in spring.

Lemon grass (*Cymbopogon citratus*) TENDER PERENNIAL

- Divide clumps in spring.

Marjoram, sweet (*Origanum marjorana*) TENDER PERENNIAL

- Grow as an annual by sowing seeds direct on the soil surface in spring; germination can be erratic.

Mint (*Mentha species*) HARDY PERENNIAL

- Divide clumps in spring or autumn, which will also help to contain its invasive growth.
- Softwood stem tip cuttings in spring.
- Rhizome cuttings in autumn – a useful method to grow plants for winter use in the kitchen.

Oregano (*Origanum vulgare*) HARDY PERENNIAL

- Divide clumps in spring or after flowering in late summer. It may be possible to remove rooted stems.
- Take softwood stem tip cuttings in summer.

Parsley (*Petroselinum crispum*) HARDY BIENNIAL

- Sow seed under cover at 18°C (64°F) in early spring or sow direct into rich soil when soil temperature is at 15°C (59°F). Germination is often erratic.

Rosemary (*Rosmarinus officinalis*) EVERGREEN SHRUB

- Softwood heel cuttings in spring.
- Semi-ripe cuttings in summer.
- Simple or mound layering in summer.

Sage (*Salvia officinalis*) EVERGREEN SHRUB

- Sow seed under cover at 15°C (59°F) in spring.
- Softwood stem tip cuttings in late spring.
- Simple layering after flowering in late summer.

Sorrel (*Rumex acetosa*) HARDY PERENNIAL

- Sow seed direct into prepared soil in spring or autumn.
- Divide clumps in spring or autumn.

Tarragon, French (*Artemesia dracunculus*) TENDER PERENNIAL

- Softwood stem tip cuttings in spring.
- Cuttings of rhizomes in spring.
- Russian tarragon (*Artemesia dracunculoides*) can be grown from seed, but the flavour is inferior.

Thyme (*Thymus species*) EVERGREEN SHRUB

- Sow seed under cover at 20°C (68°F) on the surface of the compost in spring, or outdoors at 15°C (59°F) in summer.
- Softwood stem tip cuttings in spring.
- Semi-ripe heel cuttings in summer.
- Divide in spring if plants show suitable growth habit.
- Mound layering in spring.

VEGETABLES

Even if they are technically perennial plants, the vast majority of vegetables need to be propagated each year to provide fresh stocks. Most are grown from seed and this can be bought in from seed suppliers or collected from healthy plants in the vegetable plot. Many vegetables are either harvested before flowering or the fruit is removed for eating. If you want to collect seed for the following year, remember to either leave some plants to flower or leave some fruits to mature on the plant, so that the seed can be collected, cleaned and stored.

Cabbage grown from seed

Artichoke, Globe (*Cynara scolymus*) HARDY PERENNIAL

- Remove rooted offsets in spring.
- Divide established clumps in spring, discard the woody centre and replant into well-prepared soil.

Artichoke, Jerusalem (***Helianthus tuberosus***) HARDY PERENNIAL

- Lift tubers in autumn and store. In spring, divide large tubers into 5 cm (2 in) lengths and replant into well-prepared soil.

Asparagus (***Asparagus officinalis***) HARDY PERENNIAL

- Sow seed in modules under cover at 13–16°C (55–61°F). Plant out in summer.
- Sow seed direct in spring into drills 30 cm (12 in) apart.

- Divide crowns in late winter or early spring as growth buds appear. Take care not to damage the fleshy roots, discard the woody centre and replant into well-prepared soil in a new site.

Aubergine (*Solanum melongena*) TENDER PERENNIAL

- Sow seed in modules or pots under cover at 20°C (68°F) in March. Pot on to larger pots and harden off if growing outside. They need a warm, sunny site.

Beans, Broad (*Vicia faba*) ANNUAL

- Sow seed under cover at 7°C (46°F) in late winter.
- Sow seed direct at 10 cm (4 in) stations in early spring when soil temperatures reach 7°C (46°F). Early crops can be achieved by sowing cold-tolerant varieties in autumn.

Beans, French (*Phaseolus vulgaris*) HALF-HARDY ANNUAL

- Sow seed at 12°C (52°F) under cover in pots or direct in soil under a cloche in mid spring. Sow at three week intervals up to midsummer for a continuous crop.

Beans, Runner (*Phaseolus coccineus*) TENDER PERENNIAL

- Sow seed at 12°C (52°F) under cover and transplant, or direct into prepared soil in mid spring to early summer.

Beetroot (*Beta vulgaris*) HARDY BIENNIAL

- Beetroot 'seed' is often a cluster of several seeds in a corky fruit and germinates better if washed in running water prior to sowing to remove chemical inhibitors. Sow seed direct into prepared soil at soil temperatures of 7°C (46°F) or above.
- Sow under cover at 10°C (50°F) in early spring and plant out when 5 cm (2 in) tall. Sow at three week intervals until midsummer for a continuous crop.

Broccoli, sprouting and Calabrese (*Brassica olearacea Italica group*) HARDY BIENNIAL

- Sow seed in modules, two per section, at 13°C (55°F) in early spring. Remove one if both germinate and transplant in early summer.
- Sow seed at stations into prepared soil at 13°C (55°F). Calabrese can be sown through summer for successional cropping.

Cabbage (*Brassica oleracea Capitata Group*) HARDY BIENNIAL

- Sow seed in modules or direct into a well-prepared bed. When to sow depends on the type and expected time of harvest:
  Spring cabbage: sow in late summer to early autumn
  Summer cabbage: sow in early to mid spring
  Winter cabbage: sow in late spring.

Carrot (*Daucus carota*) HARDY BIENNIAL

- Sow seed direct into prepared soil at 7°C (46°F) or above, from spring to late summer for successional crops.

Courgette, Marrow (*Cucurbita pepo*) HALF HARDY ANNUAL

- Sow seeds on their sides two per 7.5 cm (3 in) pot under cover at 15°C (59°F) in spring. Later remove the weaker seedling and plant out after the last frost.
- Sow direct, two seeds per station, in late spring.

Garlic (*Allium sativum*) HARDY BIENNIAL

- In early spring, divide a bulb into separate cloves and plant these 4 cm (1½ in) deep in well-drained soil.

Leek (*Allium porrum*) HARDY BIENNIAL

- Sow seeds under cover, singly or in pinches, at 10–15°C (50–59°F) in mid to late winter, transplanting in early summer.
- Sow seed direct into a seedbed in spring and transplant in summer.

Lettuce (*Lactuca sativa*) HALF-HARDY ANNUALS (HARDY CULTIVARS AVAILABLE)

- Sow seed into modules at 10–15°C (50–59°F) under cover from early spring and transplant when 5 cm (2 in) tall.
- Sow seed direct into drills from spring to autumn, then thin in stages to final spacing. Avoid midsummer sowing, as lettuce seeds fail to germinate at temperatures above 20–25°C (68–77°F).
- Sow hardy cultivars in late summer outdoors and protect with a cloche for winter crops.

Onion (*Allium cepa*) HARDY BIENNIAL

- Sow seed into modules at 10–15°C (50–59°F) under cover in early spring and transplant in late spring.
- Sow direct into drills in spring under a cloche, then thin to final spacing.
- Plant onion 'sets' (immature onions) singly into prepared soil in early to mid spring.

Parsnip (*Pastinaca sativa*) HARDY BIENNIAL

- Sow seed direct into prepared soil at 12°C (52°F) in early to late spring.

Seed is slow to germinate, so a quick crop of radishes sown along the same drill can act as a marker and give a quick harvest.

Pea (*Pisum sativum*) HALF-HARDY ANNUAL

- Sow two lines of seed direct into a wide drill at 10°C (50°F) in spring to early summer. Soak seed overnight to aid germination. Sow at two week intervals until midsummer for a continuous crop.

Pepper (*Capsicum annuum*) HALF-HARDY ANNUAL

- Sow in seed trays or modules under cover at 21°C (70°F) in spring.

Potato (*Solanum tuberosum*) TENDER PERENNIAL

Potatoes are stem tubers which develop underground alongside the root system. A few can be saved and replanted the following year, but they are prone to viral disease spread by aphids.

- Buy certified virus-free seed potatoes and plant from early to late spring, depending on the harvest period. Early cropping varieties are planted in early spring, maincrop potatoes later.
- Early cropping varieties can be encouraged to produce new shoots by storing in a cool, light place under cover for six weeks prior to planting. This process, called 'chitting', results in an earlier harvest.

Salad leaves (various)

A huge variety of plants can be grow to supply tender young leaves for salads. They are harvested on a 'cut and come again' principle: only a few are removed so that the plant continues to produce a fresh supply over a period of weeks.

- Sow seed into modules at 10–15°C (50–59°F) in spring to early summer and transplant to their final spacing in well-prepared soil.
- Sow seed direct into drills at 10–15°C (50–59°F) in spring to early summer. Thin only lightly, but harvest regularly. Sow at three week intervals for a continuous crop.

Spinach (*Spinacia oleracia*) HARDY ANNUAL

- Sow direct into prepared soil at 10°C (50°F) in spring to early summer and thin in stages to its final spacing. Sow at intervals for a continuous crop. Avoid sowing at above 30°C (86°F) as germination is less successful.

Sweetcorn (*Zea mays*) HALF-HARDY ANNUAL

- Sow seed in large modules at 10°C (50°F) in spring and transplant in early summer.
- Sow seed direct, two seeds per station, into well-prepared soil in spring.

Tomato (*Lycopersicon esculentum*) TENDER PERENNIAL

- Sow seed in modules at 15°C (59°F) in spring. Transplant outside after the last frosts.

FRUIT

Fruit grows on a variety of different plants, each with their own growth habit and methods of propagation. Strawberries, for example, are propagated from runners (offsets) while currants are raised from hardwood cuttings. Although it is always important to select healthy stock from which to propagate, this is especially true of fruit varieties. Over time, soft fruits can become infected with viruses which are transferred to young plants by vegetative propagation. If existing plants show signs of infection, it is advisable to buy in fresh stocks certified virus free.

Victoria plum

Tree fruits

These are generally grown on rootstocks as a result of grafting or budding. The rootstock can determine the vigour of the mature plant, offering greater opportunities to grow trained fruit trees, or trees in limited spaces.

Apple (*Malus sylvestris* var. domestica)

Apples are propagated by chip budding, T-budding or by whip and tongue grafting. The choice of rootstock is important to determine how big the tree will grow.

- **M27 (very dwarfing)** Tree grows to 1.2–2 m (4–6 ft). Use for step-over, cordon and pot-grown plants.
- **M9 (dwarfing)** Tree grows to 2–3 m (6–10 ft). Use for bush, cordon and espalier plants.
- **M26 (semi-dwarfing)** Tree grows to 2.4–3.6 m (8–12 ft). Use for bush, cordon and espalier plants.
- **MM106** Tree grows to 3.6–5.5 m (12–18 ft). Use for bush, cordon and espalier plants.
- **MM111 (semi-vigorous)** Tree grows to 4.5–6 m (15–20 ft). Use for standard and espalier plants.

Cherry (*Prunus avium*)

Cherries are propagated by chip budding, T-budding or by whip and tongue grafting, normally onto a cherry rootstock called 'Colt'.

Fig (*Ficus carica*)

Propagate by hardwood cuttings in early autumn.

Pear (*Pyrus communis* var. sativa)

Pears are propagated by chip budding, T-budding or by whip and tongue grafting onto a quince rootstock. Some varieties are incompatible with quince, so need to be first grafted onto a variety that is compatible with quince (double worked).

- **Quince C (semi-dwarfing)** Tree grows to 3 m (9 ft). Use for bush, fan, espalier and cordon plants.
- **Quince A (semi-vigorous)** Tree grows to 4 m (12 ft). Use for bush, fan, espalier and cordon plants.

Plum (*Prunus domestica*)

Plums are propagated by chip budding, T-budding or by whip and tongue grafting onto a plum rootstock.

- **Pixy (dwarfing)** Tree grows to 2 m (7 ft). Use for bush and pyramid plants.
- **St Julien A (moderately vigorous)** Tree grows to 3–4 m (9–12 ft). Use for bush, fan and pyramid plants.
- **Brompton (moderately vigorous)** Tree grows to 4.5 m (13 ft). Use for half-standard plants.

Other fruits

Blackcurrant (*Ribes nigrum*)

- Hardwood cuttings in late autumn – make cuttings 20–25 cm (8–10 in) long and insert with two buds above ground level.

Blackberry (*Rubus hybrids*)

- Tip layering in summer. Bury the stem tip in fertile soil.
- Leaf bud cuttings in summer.

Blueberry (*Vaccinium hybrids*)

- Softwood cuttings in early summer; insert in ericaceous compost.

Cranberry (*Vaccinium macrocarpon*)

- Simple layering in spring.

Gooseberry (*Ribes uva-crispa*)

- Hardwood cuttings in autumn; insert to half their depth.

Grape (*Vitis vinifera*)

- Hardwood cuttings in winter. Make cuttings 20 cm (8 in) long. Alternatively, make shorter cuttings to include one bud only (vine eye) and root at 18°C (64°F).
- Whip and tongue graft onto Vitis rootstocks, either V. berlandieri or V. rupestris.

Kiwi fruit (*Actinidia deliciosa*)

- Semi-ripe cuttings in summer. Reduce leaves by half.
- Simple layering in autumn.

Raspberry (*Rubus idaeus*)

- Divide suckers in late autumn.

Redcurrant and Whitecurrant (*Ribes sativum*)

- Hardwood cuttings in autumn. Make cuttings 30 cm (12 in) long and remove all but the top four buds. Insert to half their depth.

Strawberry (*Fragaria x ananassa*)

- Remove runners (offsets) in mid- to late summer.

GLOSSARY OF TERMS

Annual A plant that completes its life cycle (germinates from seed, flowers, sets seed and dies) within a year.

Apical bud A bud located at the tip of a growth shoot. Also known as the terminal bud.

Axil The angle formed where a leaf is attached to the main stem.

Axillary bud A bud that sits in the leaf axil between the main stem and the base of the leaf.

Auxins Naturally occurring substances produced by a plant which can influence plant growth and the tendency to promote rooting. Synthetic auxins are contained in preparations of rooting hormone.

Basal shoot A shoot that emerges from the base of the plant.

Basal cutting A cutting that is removed from the parent plant at the point where it emerges from a stem that was made in the previous season.

Bedding A plant producing bright flowers over a long period in summer on compact plants. Most cannot survive temperatures below 5°C (41°F).

Biennial A plant that completes its life cycle within two years. It germinates from seed and produces roots and leaves in the first year, then flowers, sets seed and dies in the second year.

Bottom heat Gentle heat supplied to the base of a plant or cutting to encourage rooting, by placing the container into a heated propagator or onto a heated mat.

Broadcast A method of sowing seed so that it is scattered evenly over a seed bed.

Budding A method of joining two woody plants together using the stem and root system of one and a single bud of another closely related plant.

Bud union The point at which the bud (scion) is joined to the main stem (rootstock).

Callus A protective tissue formed by the cambium to aid healing when a surface is cut or damaged.

Cambium A layer of actively dividing cells which promote growth. The cambium sits directly under the bark or rind of a stem and is responsible for increasing stem girth and forming calluses.

Crown The upper part of a rootstock from which shoots arise, sitting at or just below soil level.

Dormancy Seed: Where a viable seed fails to germinate in ideal conditions as other factors prevent it from doing so. Plant: A period when growth slows or ceases in unfavourable conditions, usually winter.

Drill A straight furrow drawn in the soil into which seed is sown thinly. It can aid seedling and weed identification when they first emerge.

Embryo A cluster of cells forming a seed shoot and root within a seed case.

Ericaceous A potting compost composed of peat or a peat alternative where the pH is adjusted to suit plants that require acid conditions to grow successfully.

F1 hybrid Plants produced by crossing two selected pure-bred parents to produce uniform, vigorous offspring. These are produced commercially for a small range of vegetables and bedding plants. The seed collected from these plants will show variations from the F1 parents.

Fruit An outer casing derived from the ovary containing one or many seeds. The fruit may be hard (eg a nut), dry and papery (eg a pea pod) or fleshy (eg a berry).

Grafting A method of propagation which joins the shoot (scion) of one plant with a stem and root system (rootstock) of another closely related plant.

Graft union The point where the scion and rootstock are joined together.

Half hardy A plant that cannot withstand temperatures lower than 0°C (37°F) and needs protection in winter.

Hardy A plant that can withstand low temperatures and can remain planted outside all year round.

Hardening off To gradually acclimatize plants to the lower temperatures of the open garden after being raised in a protected environment.

Heel A small tag of bark and tissue remaining on the base of a side stem when it is pulled away from the main stem.

Leaf bud A small bud that forms at the leaf axil.

Loam A soil containing equal proportions of sand, silt and clay.

Internodal cutting A cutting that is trimmed at the base between two nodes.

Internode The length of stem between two nodes.

Node A swelling on the stem where a leaf is attached with a dormant bud in the leaf axil.

Nursery bed A sheltered garden area, set aside for propagation before rooted plants are transplanted to their final positions.

Offset A young plant that arises from the parent at the base.

Perennial A plant that grows for more than two years. Hardy perennial: a general term referring to non-woody perennial plants that put up flower shoots from the ground each year, then die back. Woody perennial: a general term referring to plants that shoot from and extend a woody framework each year, including trees, shrubs and many climbers.

Petiole The leaf stalk that attaches the leaf to the stem.

Pollination The transfer of pollen from the anther to the stigma of a flower. Cross pollination: pollen is transferred to a flower on a different plant. Self pollination: pollen is transferred to another flower on the same plant or within the same flower.

Potting on When a plant is moved from a smaller pot to one that is slightly larger to accommodate the developing root system.

Pricking out Transferring a seedling from the compost in which it germinated to a fresh tray or pot to give it space to grow on vigorously.

Rootstock The crown and root system of a plant. Also, the main plant onto which another piece is grafted (also called the stock).

Runner A horizontal overground stem that extends from the parent plant and roots where a node touches the soil.

Scarify To damage the hard coat around a seed by abrasion or cutting to encourage germination.

Scion The piece of a plant, usually a shoot or bud, that is joined to the rootstock in the process of grafting or budding.

Seedbed An area of soil that is cultivated to a fine tilth and set aside for raising plants from seed before transplanting to their final positions.

Stock Another term for the rootstock used in grafting and budding.

Stratify To expose seed to a period of low or high temperatures after sowing to overcome dormancy.

Successional sowing Sowing seed of a quickly maturing crop at regular intervals to achieve a harvestable crop over a longer period.

Sucker A shoot that arises below the soil from a plant's stem or root.

Tender A plant that cannot withstand temperatures below 5°C (41°F) without damage.

Tilth The crumb size of a compost or soil. It needs to be fine to be suitable for seed germination.

Transplant To move a plant from a seedbed or nursery bed to its final position. Also, a plant that is to be moved.

Wound To remove a sliver of bark from the base of a cutting to encourage rooting.

INDEX